the
Song
of Songs

Books by M. Basil Pennington

The Monks of Mount Athos: A Western Monk's Extraordinary
    Spiritual Journey on Eastern Holy Ground

Finding Grace at the Center: The Beginning of Centering Prayer

An Invitation to Centering Prayer

Centering Prayer

Centered Living

Call to the Center: The Gospel's Invitation to Deeper Prayer

A Place Apart: Monastic Prayer and Practice for Everyone

Awake in the Spirit: A Personal Handbook of Prayer

Lectio Divina: Renewing the Ancient Practice of Praying the Scriptures

Lessons from the Monastery That Touch Your Life

Listening: God's Word for Today

Living in the Question

Seeking His Mind: 40 Meetings with Christ

Poetry as Prayer

Retreat with Thomas Merton

Thomas Merton, My Brother: His Journey to Freedom, Compassion
    and Final Integration

True-Self/False-Self: Unmasking the Spirit Within

the Song of Songs

A SPIRITUAL COMMENTARY

Meditations by
Abbot M. Basil Pennington, ocso

Illustrations by Phillip Ratner

Walking Together, Finding the Way
SKYLIGHT PATHS Publishing
Woodstock, Vermont

The Song of Songs:
A Spiritual Commentary

2004 First Printing
Text © 2004 by the Cistercian Abbey of Spencer, Inc.
Illustrations © 2004 by Phillip Ratner

Library of Congress Cataloging-in-Publication Data
Pennington, M. Basil.
The Song of Songs : a spiritual commentary / drawings by Phillip Ratner ; meditations by M. Basil Pennington.
p. cm.
ISBN 1-59473-004-0
1. Bible. O.T. Song of Solomon—Commentaries. I. Title.
BS1485.53.P42 2004
223'.9077—dc22

                                     2004006856

10 9 8 7 6 5 4 3 2 1

Jacket Design: Tim Holtz

Manufactured in Canada

SkyLight Paths Publishing is creating a place where people of different spiritual traditions come together for challenge and inspiration, a place where we can help each other understand the mystery that lies at the heart of our existence.

SkyLight Paths sees both believers and seekers as a community that increasingly transcends traditional boundaries of religion and denomination—people wanting to learn from each other, *walking together, finding the way.*

SkyLight Paths, "Walking Together, Finding the Way" and colophon are trademarks of LongHill Partners, Inc., registered in the U.S. Patent and Trademark Office.

Walking Together, Finding the Way
Published by SkyLight Paths Publishing
A Division of LongHill Partners, Inc.
Sunset Farm Offices, Route 4, P.O. Box 237
Woodstock, VT 05091
Tel: (802) 457-4000 Fax: (802) 457-4004
www.skylightpaths.com

To the Monks of the
Abbey of Our Lady of Holy Spirit

Men of the Spirit—Men of Prayer
Men who seek to be kissed by the Kiss of his mouth

Moments

Welcome

*D*elight—that is what this Song of Songs, this greatest Song of all Songs, is about. Or rather this wondrous collection of songs. We do not know who brought this delight-filled collection together, or when, or where. Commentators of later centuries have tried to discern a drama here, or a narrative or story, but it takes some doing so to discern. If these ancient love songs have anything that draws them into one beyond the Spirit who inspired the redactor, it is the recurrence of certain words, phrases, sentences, and images. But essentially it is their theme, it is their inner spirit, it is their ever-breathless aspirations of love. Verse by verse they speak to what is deepest in us; they give voice to our own unutterable aspirations. They call forth what is deepest in us.

For much of two thousand years, Jewish and Christian men and women of the Spirit—thinkers, pray-ers, and mystics—have experienced these songs as speaking of a love intensely human and more, as a love sacramental of the greatest of love affairs, that of God for his People, his People of both Covenants. It was with a little more hesitation that they saw them giving expression to the love of the individual for God and God's love for the individual. But the greatest of the commentators, Maimonides and Bernard of Clairvaux, and their disciples readily saw the Song of Songs in this way and were enchanted, encouraged, and delighted by what they saw.

Can you separate the individual from the People? Are the People anything other than the chosen individuals called together to be a People? Thus, as we enter into the realm of the Song we are individuals and a People. We know the stirrings of a completely human love—sensuous, erotic, passionate—and we know that it finds its fullest expression only in our romance with the Divine; its ultimate realization and consummation can only be found there. We invite the Spirit who breathes in the words and finds some expression in the extraordinary drawings of Phillip Ratner to call us forth and lead us into the experience of this love for which we crave, which alone can satisfy.

To find in a sacred song of the Hebrew Bible—sometimes called the Old Testament—the mystical richness of the new Revelation in Christ Jesus may seem to some like putting new wine in old wineskins (Mark 2:22). But it is not. The sacred, inspired Scriptures are never old. They are ever new with all the vitality of their divine inspiration, ever ready to expand with the effervescence of the Divine Spirit. At the same time they never lose the exquisite beauty of their literal meaning. They are love songs of the most passionate sort, filled with imagery that seeks to express all the enthusiasm of a tumultuous passion. Meditators on these inspired words ever perceive Ezekiel's wheels within wheels within wheels as one inviting insight circles around another—not old and new, but a whirling of countless lights celebrating an ever-present love, a love that is beyond all expression and inspires all the inadequate exaggerations of human expression, the mysticism of a divine love enfolded in the gauzy veil of ecstatic human passion.

We might look upon the Song of Songs as a multidimensional hologram: meanings within meanings within meanings. In recent times, some scripture scholars have spoken of the *sensus plenior* (the fuller sense), a meaning beyond the literal meaning of the text, a meaning intended by God in inspiring the sacred writer. The Fathers of the Church in the early centuries of Christian experience defined a fourfold sense of Scripture: the literal; the allegorical (perhaps not too different from the *sensus plenior*); the moral, that to which the Text calls us; and ultimately the anagogical or unitive sense, that to which the Sacred Text ultimately points. In the twelfth century, William of St. Thierry wrote his *Exposition on the Song of Songs,* seeking to bring out the moral sense. In his introduction he said he would leave the exploration of the richer, more mysterious allegorical sense to his friend and master, Bernard of Clairvaux. Bernard, in his eighty-six sermons on the first thirty-five verses of the Song, in fact explored all the different senses.

In its literal sense the Song is obviously dramatic poetry presenting a passionate love affair. Authors through the centuries have found a *sensus plenior,* seeing in the poetry something of the story of God's love for his Chosen People. Christians have often identified the Lover with Christ, God incarnate, and they see the Beloved as the Church or the individual.

A difficulty men have had (and I do mean "men" here—most commentators have been men) with allegorizing this love poetry to depict the love of God for the individual is that the Beloved is a young woman. Isaiah the Prophet sees the beloved of God as both male and female, as bridegroom and bride:

> I exalt for joy in Yahweh, my soul rejoices in my God,
> for he has clothed me in garments of salvation,
> he has wrapped me in a cloak of saving justice,
> like a bridegroom wearing his garland,
> like a bride adorned in her jewels.
>
> —*Isaiah 61:10*

In the Song of Songs God's poet seeks to bedeck the groom and the bride with the greatest possible beauty, not only accidentally with jewels and crown, but intrinsically with a beauty of body and soul that is beyond description and must be glimpsed only thorough a maze of metaphors.

The text of Isaiah reminds us that God, through his inspired writers, chose again and again to use what should be the most beautiful and complete union between humans as the image of the union God wants with his People, "As a bridegroom rejoices in his bride, so will your God rejoice in you" (Isaiah 62:5). It is of little wonder, then, that insightful commentators through the centuries repeatedly saw this as the deeper message of this inspired and inspiring collection of love songs. Our fulfillment is found as one with the People—and yet we never lose our individuality. We are individuals uniquely created and loved by God. Hence commentators, especially those of a more mystical bent, quickly found in these inspired poems the story also of God's love for each one of us.

In our meditations we move freely through the different levels of this beautiful multidimensional hologram, enjoying whatever insights we receive as they come along. Our hero is the ideal Lover, the model, who is a king like unto the greatest, Solomon, the King of Peace, the King of Jerusalem, City of Peace, the eternal city, the new Jerusalem, coming down from above. Yet, he is the Lord, the God who espouses to himself a People, a Chosen People, the sons and daughters of Abraham, but in truth, all the sons and daughters of God, the whole human family, called into ultimate unity in the eternal Omega, and each and every individual within the People; indeed, the writer himself. The young maiden is the ravishing Beloved of the ideal Lover. She is the Beloved People God has chosen as his own. She is the Church, the People of God chosen in Christ; she is the individual being romanced by God, the mystics of all the ages, the lovers of today, and that fairest of all God's creatures, the holy Virgin of Nazareth, the Mother of the Lord. As the meditations progress it would be literarily and grammatically disconcerting if this hologramatic optic were not present to help us experience the stance move fluidly from one image to another as the Lover, the eternal God, the Lord, speaks to and is addressed by the Beloved, the People of God, the Church, the Virgin Mary, the individual, even the writer. We are caught up in the unified and unifying force of love that hurtles the whole of the creation project toward its ultimate fullness in the eternal Omega. This reality is witnessed to by the fact that a traditional Jewish artist and a traditional Christian contemplative, both coming out of the fullness of their respective traditions, can sense a profound unity within their expressions that blend to create this volume.

The images our poets draw upon in these songs may indeed seem strange to us. We are used to metaphors that draw on the more obvious similitudes. The Hebrew reaches to deeper qualities. A familiarity with the Psalms, the primary book of Hebrew poetry so familiar to every son and daughter of Abraham, and with those other collections ascribed to Solomon, Proverbs, and Ecclesiastes, may help us to be more in tune with the poetic imagery of these love songs, to appreciate the rich harmonies to which they give voice.

This is not a scholarly commentary or in fact any kind of commentary on the Sacred Text. It is rather a rumination. The Fathers like to speak of our being nourished by Sacred Scripture like a "clean animal." The cow or some other such animal first goes out and eats of the rich pasture. Then it settles under a tree and regurgitates what it has eaten to further chew the cud—a process that will eventually produce the milk of prayer and the cream of contemplation. Here we offer our rumination in image and word, hoping that it will enable you to share it and enjoy the milk and cream, prayer and contemplative delight.

Phillip Ratner's ecstatic drawings incite us to leave the narrow parameters of rational thought to enter into a transcendent experience of the text. It is my hope that my poor words might facilitate this. I am very grateful to Phil for allowing me to share in this volume with him. Since my first days in the monastery fifty years ago, I have delved into this sublime text, aided by the Cistercian Fathers; Bernard of Clairvaux, William of St. Thierry, Gilbert of Hoyland, and John of Ford, as well as earlier Fathers such as Ambrose of Milan, Gregory of Nyssa, and Gregory the Great. I keep my text short so as not to lead you too far away from the more enticing and expressive drawings. Do not hesitate to record your own feelings, thoughts, and inspirations. But do not get caught up in words. They are products of our very limited minds. Rather, let the drawings draw and the Sacred Text invite you to realms beyond words.

This volume is meant for contemplation. Again, it is not a commentary—far from it. It is but a sharing of some of what this celebration of love has evoked in the soul of an artist and a contemplative, a layman and a monk, a Jew and a Christian, in the hope that it might invite you, a fellow traveler, to take some time to let this poetry play on the chords of your own heart and evoke currents of delight. The love of which it sings belongs to you. You are the Beloved of the Divine Lover. You are loved with a love beyond that which human words can express, which song and pen seek in some way to convey or at least hint at. Let go. Let the currents of love invade you. Let your deepest soul rejoice as it is drawn forth into the ecstasy of love: Oh, give me the kisses of your mouth!

The translation of the Song of Songs offered here is my own—save for those within the drawings themselves, which are those of my artist friend—and is influenced no doubt by the many others I have savored. All translators will concur: there are many words woven into the fabric of these songs that mystify us in their uniqueness. In creating an English text we can sometimes only make what we hope is an educated guess, knowing that the guesses of other knowledgeable translators are equally if not more justifiable. We can only aim at a certain consonance and sense as we blend the harmonies of rich analogies. How much of the delight of the original songs is lost? We can only hope that under the inspiration of the Spirit most of it is ours as we enter into this realm of love and let the actors play on our deepest heartstrings. The resonance of the very first words of the Song is enough to set us off forever: Oh, give me the kisses of your mouth!

The Song of Songs

The title is not simply "Song" but "Song of Songs," a detail not without significance. For though I have read many songs in Scripture, I cannot recall any that bear such a name.... It is a special divine impulse that inspired these songs of Solomon's that now celebrate the praises of Christ and his Church, the gift of holy love, the sacrament of endless union with God. Here too are expressed the mounting desires of the soul, its marriage song, as exultation of spirit poured forth in figurative language pregnant with delight.... Accordingly, because of its excellence, I consider this nuptial song to be well deserving of the title that so remarkably designates it, the Song of Songs....

—Bernard of Clairvaux, *Sermons on the Song of Songs*, 1:7

"The Song of Songs"

Song of Songs

*I*t needs to be said more than once. One speaking is not enough. It is *the* Song. *The* Song of all songs—for it is the Song of Love.

The lips do not move in this speaking. The eyes do not see. The ears do not hear. They are lost in higher levels of being.

Presence is enough. Indeed, it is all. "My Loved One is mine and I am his" (Song 2:16). The word is spoken. Our whole being is the word.

Soon enough it will be time for words. The tides swell up within us and demand expression. "My heart pours forth the good word" (Psalm 44:1). But not yet.

Let the Presence be. Let the celestial music sound in our ears. Let the Divine Word swirl around us, a mystic vision, too much an expression of the Divine—for this is Love. God is Love. It is a Word too great, too full, too sublime, too rich, too transcendent to be captured by any eye.

It seems like the clouds, folding and unfolding, expressing themselves in shapes, millions upon millions, never ceasing—yet, a Cloud of Unknowing. "For this knowledge is too great for me; it is beyond all understanding" (Psalm 139:6).

Perhaps it is but the flutter of angels' wings. They know. They see. They hover. They fly. The Cherubim. The Seraphim. They hide even as they reveal. They proclaim the Presence even as they protect our poor human eyes from the Vision too great. This is Love.

Do we hear celestial words? Is it the ten-stringed harp of Jesse's son? Or the harps of a heavenly choir? The sound of Love—it does not cause the tympanum of human ear to vibrate, but the whole of our being vibrates. Love is the music of being. It is music written in heaven. It is the music of God himself. It is God. God is love.

The eye does not see. The ear does not hear (Isaiah 64:3). The lips do not move—they do not need to move. But can they long stay apart—these pairs of longing lips?

The serenity is so deceptive. The communication is so powerful. It reaches to my deepest being, to my outermost extremities. My very toes sense this movement of Love. How long can I be in it and not be totally lost in a swell of passion?

"My Loved One is mine and I am his" (Song 2:16).

The Song of Songs indeed. My whole being sings it, is caught up in it, is it. My being sings love, for it is love, love to the Lover.

The beginning is in the end; the end is in the beginning. No journey is seriously undertaken—not even a journey of love—without the end in view. What other end can there be for a journey of love than that the Beloved should be covered with the kisses of the Lover. In the journey of life, the Divine Lover. For what else is life but a journey of love—from the launch of love in the womb to the consummation of love in the tender intimacy of the eternal Divine Embrace, to the mingling of the Spirit who is love.

No mere meeting of minds is desired. Memories are not enough. Nor is even the oneness of will sufficient even if most basic. Only a complete and essential union, a transforming union, a divinizing union brought about by a sharing of Spirit. We do not know how to pray—to commune with the Divine—as we ought, but Holy Spirit, the Kiss of Father and Son, prays within us—brings about the communion that alone satisfies all the aspirations of love that breathe within us (Romans 8:26).

It is a song meant to be played on a ten-stringed harp—on the five senses of a harmonious pair. Nothing less than the confluence of sight, sound, smell, taste, and touch can begin to express the totality of this communion. We would savor the Divine, seeing in faith, hearing the word of Revelation, enjoying the scent of things beyond us, longing for the touch that will transform. This is a song that seeks to evoke every sensuous experience of the human and still knows that it falls so far short of the Divine. And nothing short of the Divine will satisfy. It is of this we sing in the Song of Songs: the total reality of human love as a sacrament of the still greater and more ecstatic love.

The harp may play like unto the flutter of angels' wings; the harmonies may indeed be inspired by the Divine Spirit; yet, as long as the words are those of human lips they fall far short. They cannot bridge the gap. The whole call of being is for communion, for union. That is what this Song of Songs says. It sums up all the aspirations of every movement of love that ever gave voice to itself in song. And yet, in a moment of highest realization it speaks by silence, face to face, being to being. Words will come. It will seek to express the inexpressible. It will call forth image upon image in an almost chaotic plethora, and yet ever remain dissatisfied. In dream and vision it will seek beyond itself; in ecstasy it will seek fulfillment. It will faint, it will languish, and yet it will ever seek. It will know consummation. And ever want more. This song embraces the richness of every song of love and yet ever wants more to express a love that necessarily embraces all expression and yet remains inexpressible. It is the Song of Songs.

Kiss Me

Oh, give me the kisses of your mouth
for your love is more delightful than wine,
the scent of the best of ointments.
Your name is a wafted scent—no wonder the maidens love you.
Draw me!
We will run after you!
The King has brought me into his storerooms.
We shall rejoice and exult in you;
we remember your breasts better than wine;
how rightly you are loved!
I am black but beautiful, Daughters of Jerusalem,
like the tents of Kedar, like the tent curtains of Solomon.
Stare not at me because I am dark, because the sun has colored me.
My mother's sons were angry with me;
they made me keeper of the vineyards,
but my own vineyard I have not kept!
Show me, you whom my soul loves, where you pasture,
where you lie down at noon;
lest I begin to wander among the flocks of your companions.
If you do not know yourself, O beautiful one among women,
Go and follow the tracks of the flock
and pasture your kids beside tents of the shepherds.

—Song of Songs 1:2–9

"Oh, give me the kisses of your mouth
for your love is more delightful than wine."

1:2

OH, give me of the kisses of your
mouth, for your love is
more delightful than WINE...

Kiss Me

O h, give me—give me—give me. The thirst cries out from the deepest depths of my belly.

Oh, give me the kisses of your mouth. Not one. But kiss me again and again.

Let the touch of your love, the breath of your love invade me. My whole being thirsts for you.

Ah, your lips were lips ever made more delectable by the blood of the grape. Intoxicating love, the touch of your lips. Searing lips, lips that set me afire.

Give me the kisses. Let them burn my lips even as the savor sends torrents of delight through my being. No chalice was ever so filled, nor ever did a chalice have such a thirst to be filled. Bottomless is my cup in its thirst for your love. For you are Love—my Love. "My Loved One is mine and I am his" (Song 2:16). May your intoxicating lips press upon the lips of my soul the ravishing love that you are.

These grapes need not be crushed to fill the cup. Your lips need only to press against mine, and the sweetest of wine—the most intoxicating—takes hold of my spirit. No other lips can so inflame, so inebriate, as these lips of yours, for you are Love.

Lips so soft, so tender, lips made for kissing—how you ravish me. I want only their delicate touch again and again. They need but brush my eager lips and I know paroxysms of love. Love touches; I am all love. Can it be so?

I want those soft and tender lips to press me hard. I want them to devour me. I want our lips to be but one set of lips, my lips wholly lost in your lips. No need to bite or chew or grab or suck. I yield willingly. I long for nothing more. Kiss me with the kiss of your lips.

Yes, wine—the finest wine. No wine was ever like this. From your lips comes a love that makes my heart pound, my head swirl. I have drunk what I have thought to be the finest wines: the rich blood-red of Burgundy, the warmth of Frascatti, the Rosé d'Anjou, "the best wine in the world." I have known the love of woman, passionate, hot, tender, caring; I have known the love of man, strong, virile, totally possessive; I have known the bright-eyed innocent love of a child—oh, how it has melted my heart. But no love is like unto your love, for you are Love.

For this Love I do not give up other loves. They no longer exist. They are all taken up into this Love. The delight in your Love leaves no room for any other delight. There can be nothing more, nothing besides. It is all here.

It is a light, this Love of yours, that makes all else shine until it delights and is lost in your delight.

Intoxicate me, Lips of Love, with the press of your Love, a kiss beyond all kisses. O Breath of Love, sweetest savor, you dilate my every cell. No part of me escapes this delightful fire. Kiss me, again, again, and again. And let the burning wave inundate my body and my soul. For your Love is totally ravishing. Your lips, their touch, set off this current of hottest pleasure. Give me your kisses. Give me your kisses—this is the cry of my whole being, even if I open not my mouth. For this wine is the wine of the Spirit that needs no cup, no word, only the touch of Love.

Do not hold back. Do not delay. Do not cease. Kisses of your mouth, this is my whole being's longing. The one who drinks of this, thirsts yet more (John 4:13). I can never have enough of your love, of you who are Love.

Actions speak louder than words! I believe in your love; I hope with all my being that our love will be consummated in complete union. Act now! Kiss me with the kiss of your mouth.

Give yourself to me, lips to lips, breathing the very Breath of your love into me—a holy communion. Let me feel, smell, taste, touch your Love. I want to experience your Love, the experience that will set my whole being on fire, that will warm my whole being with undulating currents of delight. For this I live. For this my whole being longs. For this was I made and continue to exist. Without this experience of love my being is as good as dead. Without a hope of this there is no meaning to my continued existence. Kiss me with the kiss of your mouth.

What is the Kiss of your mouth? It is where the human and divine become completely one. It is the Kiss of God for humanity. It is the Kiss of God for his People, the consummation of his creation in incarnation. It is the Word on the Divine Lips that expresses all that is God in human form. It is the God-man.

Longing for total fulfillment, can this ever be ours that we, the very image of our Divine Creator, be oned with our Maker, who has made us not only like God's self but for God's self? And can we ever find this save within God's People? For our Creator Lover embraces in one great embrace all God's creation.

How much we struggle with the belief that you, the Divine Lover, really love this poor little human, so plagued with sin and infidelity, weakness and impurities of every sort. Oh, give me the kisses of your mouth! Does the very fact that I long for this mean that he, too, longs for it? From whence comes this ardent desire for a ravishing experience of the Unknown? Can I truly believe that the love that knows nothing of reverence can so bypass all the realms of propriety that the most Exalted Love should bend low to kiss such as I? The faith that grounds a hope, the hope that grounds a faith, makes the love audacious beyond all reason and decorum. Oh, give me the kisses of your mouth! Does the lowest, the last, the least aspire to the Kiss of the Kiss? Yes! Give me the kisses of your mouth! My whole being aspires only because your Spirit has inspired, has breathed through my being, with all the currents of Divine Love. I would live in this longing, powerful though it be, rather than try to exist in some way without it.

Lily among Thorns

To a steed among Pharaoh's chariots would I liken you, my
    Beloved:
Your cheeks are beautiful like turtle doves, your neck as jewels.
We will make for you pendants of gold inlaid with silver.
While the king was on his couch, my nard gave forth its fragrance.
A sachet of myrrh is my Loved One to me;
he shall abide between my breasts.
A cluster of henna blossoms is my Loved One to me
in the vineyards of En-gedi.
Ah, you are fair, my Darling. Ah, you are fair with your dove-like
    eyes!
Ah, you are beautiful, my Dear One—our bed is fresh and green.
The beams of our house are cedar; our rafters, cypress.
I am a flower of the fields, a lily of the valley.
Like a lily among thorns is my Darling among the maidens.

—*Song of Songs 1:9–2:2*

"Like a lily among thorns
is my Darling among the maidens."

כְּשׁוֹשַׁנָּה בֵּין
הַחוֹחִים כֵּן
רַעְיָתִי בֵּין
הַבָּנוֹת׃

Like a Lily among thorns
so is my darling among the maidens
2:2

phillip ratner

Lily among Thorns

*E*nraptured Lover! One exclamation of love follows the other. At first so much the imagery of a man, from the male mind: A great steed, the greatest, chosen to draw the great king's chariot—what could be more beautiful? Jewels of all sorts, rich and inlaid, adorning the most beautiful. But then the tenderness of romance begins to soften and become gentle: what can draw one more than gentle beckoning eyes? Yes, the drawing is to the couch, verdant, ready for love, protected and scented by cedar and cypress.

But the Beloved would find yet a better simile: a flower of the fields, the lily of the valley. It bespeaks a fragile beauty, one to be handled with care, yet resplendent: not even Solomon in all his royal robes was clothed like one of these (Matthew 6:29).

Yes, says our Lover, a lily—and such a lily that all others seem to be but thorns in comparison: dry, dark, piercing. Under the nourishing warmth of Love, bedewed by grace, the Beloved comes forth from the stalk, gently expands and turns radiantly white, opens and gives forth her enthralling scent, expands, fully blossoms, fruitful with colorful stamen and pistil, yet ever so delicate, so susceptible to the piercing jealousy of others.

Yet, the Beloved is surrounded by companions, devoted and loving, who use their sharpness to protect—at least if they are true to their better selves. It is for her to blossom as the unique beauty, the delight of her Lover.

Lover of my soul, can I believe you so look upon me?

I live and grow, indeed, among thorns. But they are not all protectors. Some are loyal, loving, and protective. But others are jealous, spiteful, and revengeful. They tear me and rip me. I feel shredded and bedraggled. I have not the pure and unspotted whiteness of the lily. The odor I give forth is not wholly a heavenly scent. I am stained by sin and give off the malodor of sin.

Yet, in reality my Lover still sees me as the lily among thorns. He would make me strong like a magnificent steed. He would adorn me with jewels that would cover and hide my stains and tares. He would look into my eyes and see the love that is there in their depths. He would invite me into his verdant hideaway beneath the cedars and cypresses. And there in a mystical embrace he would make love to me.

Such is my Lover. His eyes of love are such that I remain his lily among thorns, so special am I to him, so healing and wholing and beautifying is his love for me. Under his beneficent gaze I can open out and give forth a beautiful odor that will delight all.

There is no condemnation of the thorns, even as they turn in and seem to come at me from every side. Can the jealousy and spite and anger and vengefulness of others truly hurt me? Not in the eyes of my Lover. They only enhance my true beauty. He himself was pierced from every side, even those who ate bread with him (Psalm 41:9), Divine Bread, abandoned him, denied him, even turned against him. They crowned his head with thorns (Mark 15:17). Yet, in the end he rose above all this and reigns. He readily appreciates love and celebrates a lily among thorns. For the lily, under his beneficent gaze, will yet rise higher and blossom forth and enrapture with her beauty and scent.

Look and see: is there any beauty like unto my beauty?

Does any blossom compare to it: so brilliant, so white, the very purity of light, the blending of every color, the synthesis of all that delights the eye. Its very form and shape trumpet its beauty. Its golden life-giving qualities are delicately held within. Her heart, its center, is ready to receive the seed of life.

With power that is yet delicate, it sends forth its odor of unmingled sweetness. Such a delight is the Beloved among the thorns of this world.

For long it lay so hidden, a solid bulb buried in mud, taking in the nourishment that would enable it to respond enthusiastically, as it were, to the warming radiance of the Sun of Justice. How quickly it springs up. Before the thorns can crowd in and crush, free from all fear, responding only to the attraction of the radiance of Love, it bravely bursts forth amid the thorns.

Does not the Lover take delight in his Beloved? Her beauty is such that all are indeed but dry thorns in comparison—painful obstructions that inhibit his freedom to be with and take delight in the Beloved alone. With all their worldly cares, with all their menacing needs, they seem to be intent upon engulfing the delicate beauty. It seems so fragile, and it is. It can be so easily choked and have its beauty crushed if it is not wholly intent upon responding to Love, rising resolutely above all the flitting concerns of this earthly garden.

This fairest of blossoms has little hope of so rising if it has not nourished itself well in the humility of hiddenness, in a willingness to abide the Lover's time. Only when the warmth of the Lover's radiance beckons can the Beloved hope to leap forth and rise up to drink in all the warmth and to blossom unharmed.

Gaze upon the lily. Open every pore to its beauty. Little wonder that this flower comes forth at the time of Resurrection. Hold in your hand a dry bulb, and wonder that such beauty can almost instantly burst forth from it. No matter who we are, how dry and ugly and marred and scared we see ourselves to be, we know that because we are the Beloved, when the pervading warmth of Love reaches us, we can blossom as a lily among thorns and radiate the very beauty of the Lover.

Like an Apple Tree

Like an apple tree among the trees in the forest,
so is my Loved One among the youths.
I delight to sit in his shade, and his fruit is sweet to my mouth.
He brings me into a banquet hall; he spreads over me a canopy of
    love.
Buoy me up with flowers, compass me about with apples,
for I languish with love.
His left hand under my head, his right shall embrace me.
I adjure you, Daughters of Jerusalem, by the gazelles and does of
    the field,
do not arouse, do not awaken love until it pleases.

—Song of Songs 2:3–7

"Like an apple tree among the trees in the forest,
so is my Loved One among the youths.
I delight to sit in his shade,
and his fruit is sweet to my mouth."

Like an apple TREE among trees in
the forest.
So is my beloved among the youths
I delight to sit in his shade,
And his fruit is sweet to my
mouth.

2:3

Like an Apple Tree

What a wondrous garden planted for us—yes, for us. Paradise was to be the home of us all. We were made to be God's delight, to delight in God. Only one tree did the Lord, so loving and generous, reserve to be God's own. It was of course an apple tree—not the tallest or most stately. The Son of Man would say: Learn of me, for I am meek and humble of heart (Matthew 11:29). Not the most stately but one of enchanting beauty that blossoms forth in the springtime. One of rich fruitfulness as its sweet, crisp, ruddy fruit delights the eye, the touch, and the odor with its homey warmth and welcoming security.

This fruitful tree is the Lord's presence in our midst. Not for us to grab and enviously eat. No, but for us to savor a nourishing sweetness to be ours in the restful hours of contemplation spent in his overshadowing.

This delightful fruit is no long-awaited harvest. It is the fruit of the springtime of life, when the year is still young. Not bent with long years but in the uplifting reach of a powerful youth, my Lover spreads fruitful branches over me, inviting me in turn to reach for the sweetest of fruit even as I sit in the quiet of his overshadowing.

The wonder of contemplative love: even as it rests in raptured embrace—the most satisfying, complete, and total of rest—it yet knows the sweetest of fruits. How can I not be totally delighted as I am totally fulfilled? In his embraces the Beloved knows the complete satisfaction of all her desires, even as she shares in his fruitfulness.

The Blessed Fruit of her womb (Luke 1:42) is the Fruit of the Eternal Generation, so that all generations call her blessed

(Luke 1:48). Yes, blessed among women (Luke 1:42)—but not only her. Truly God's mercy is from generation unto generation (Luke 1:50), so that all who embrace the Will of the Father is mother to this Blessed Fruit (Matthew 12:49)

True contemplation though it be, the virginal beatitude of the pure of heart is yet the most fruitful of human endeavors— indeed, not an endeavor but a reflective being. For such purity of heart sees God (Matthew 5:8) and is like God (1 John 3:2).

Though all the trees of the forest, all the delights and all the threats of the forest crowd around, yet, sitting in contemplation and nourished by the Divine, my delight is in no way distracted or threatened. Let all else be; I know only the sweetness of his fruit. And if my mouth is called upon to give utterance it can only speak sweetly of delight. No effort of mine brings it forth. It is the fruit of his delight in me and mine in him. My heart bursts forth with a good word from the delight of him (Psalm 45:1). He is too great to be encased in a heart no matter how expanded. A word that may be recorded like the word of a faithful scribe (Psalm 45:1), but more: it is one with the creative Word that is written in the creation as the Word calls it forth to an ever-greater fullness. It moves forward eagerly toward the embracing oneness of the eternal Omega.

I sit. I renounce my restless running about, my striving to be creative on my own—to possess, to capture as my own something of his fruitfulness. Rather, I sit in his shadow. I acknowledge that all is of him. I delight in this. All honor and glory is my Loved One's. His fruit is sweet to my mouth. I need not make it my own. My mouth need not vaunt my own praises. I delight in the humility of truth, in the truth of humility. I can sit in total delight. I no longer need to do or to have. I no longer need to be concerned about what others think of me. I sit in the delight of perfect contemplation. All things are mine and I am his and he is God's (1 Corinthians 3:23).

My Love, my Love, unique among all lovers—your delicate blossoms give delight to the springtime forest still so barren, giving the scent of hope, promising the fruit to come. A fruitful love is yours, delightful to the eye, smooth to the touch, nourishing in its taste, a scent that is hearty and sweet. Where better in all the forest of this world can I sit in contemplative repose than under your shadow, knowing that all my longings will be fulfilled.

Yes, my Lover promises a communion. By his fruit I am nourished and sustained, even as I long for so much more. Nourished am I unto eternal life.

I must not let the great trees overshadow me, not let their darksome shadows frighten me away. If I but sit quietly beneath your shadow, no other can ever harm me or frighten me away. Your overshadowing so fills me with delight that I can attend to naught else. In you I have all, the fruit that fills me with all sweetness. Nothing more can I desire than to remain ever hidden in your shadow, where no evil can befall.

Is this not in truth a banqueting hall? Is not his shadow in truth a banner of love, a canopy spread over me, claiming me wholly as his own?

Lover, do captivate me with the dainties of your love. Refresh me with your wondrous apples. Nourish me so that I can sustain the onslaughts of such love. Such am I, so does the passion of love draw out my whole being—all my mind, heart, soul, and strength—I can only be love, but I must be sustained and ever refreshed to be such a love for you.

Love, let your very hand sustain me. More, let your very hand press me close to your own heart. This is what I want. This is all I want. In this I want to abide. May no one or no thing ever intrude upon this most holy embrace. Here may I abide (Psalm 37:18). May this best part never be taken from me (Luke 10:42). Let the Marthas take care, the daughters of the house. I only want to be the Beloved.

The apple tree is indeed little among the lofty trees of the forest. The Divine Lover came as a humble villager, but he was fruitful. He lived by the labor of his hands. And then he went about doing good: feeding the hungry, healing the sick, giving sight to the blind (Matthew 11:5). To those who would sit at his feet, his word brought the sweetness of hope into their lives. More, he would lead them into the intoxicating cellars of Divine Love; he would teach them the self-giving ways of true love. The banner over those Loved Ones who would follow his way would be love: "See how they love one another."

He Comes

Hark! My beloved, here he comes,
Leaping over mountains,
Bounding over hills.

—Song of Songs 2:8

Let us observe the discreet and circumspect leapings of the
Bridegroom, how, both among angels and ourselves, he leaps
among the humble and bounds over the proud, for though the
Lord is high he has respect for the lowly but the haughty he regards
only from afar (Ps 137:6). Let us attend to this so as to make sure
we prepare ourselves for the redemptive leapings of the
Bridegroom, for fear that if he perceives us to be unworthy of his
visitation, he may also pass us by....

—Bernard of Clairvaux, Sermons on the Song of Songs, 54:7

"Hark! My beloved, here he comes,
leaping over mountains,
bounding over hills."

Hark my beloved! There he comes, Leaping over mountains, Bounding over hills.

phillip valie 2:8

He Comes

Alas, not all the shadows we know are the friendly shadows cast by the scented and fruitful boughs of the apple tree. Lowering clouds can frighten and chill us. Dark moments—indeed we have known them: betrayal, exile, deportation, holocaust—can kill the spirit. Prison wires have seemed far more impeding than any mountains in Israel. How very far God seems at times. Our sense is that he has turned away and fled (Song 5:6). What mountainous obstacles our own sins seem to create: our attachments, our addictions. Can a Divine Lover want to approach, regard, cherish one made so ugly by such perversions of our human nature?

However, these may not be the real mountains but simply hills. Are not the great mountains that impede the approach of the Divine Lover our lack of desire, our not wanting, our indifference, our pride? "All the day I stretch out my hands" (Isaiah 65:2). He sat upon the hill above Jerusalem. Having leaped across all the domains of creation, he sat there and wept as a mother, as a lover: "How I longed to gather you together as a hen gathers her chicks under her wings, and you refused!" (Matthew 23:37).

Nothing, absolutely nothing stops the advances of our Divine Lover. No matter how dark it may be when the night is in the midst of its course, the almighty Word leaps down (Wisdom 18:14–15). Planets, galaxies, black holes, quarks—nothing, absolutely nothing impedes the Lover, the Merciful One, the Love. In fact, when the night seems darkest and the mountainous obstacles seem greatest, that is when the Lover is indeed coming into our lives, ready to make a difference, the transforming difference love can make when its shafts of light break through the dark clouds.

Oh, the power, the wonder, the magnanimity of this Lover. His Chosen People wandered in the desert in more ways than one; yet, when Moses went up the Mount of Horeb he brought back the mercy of the Lover (Exodus 32); when he prayed with outstretched arms on the hill above the plains of battle he brought victory (Exodus 17:8–13). Century after century, when pagan emperors would crush, when infidel hordes swept down, when hatred possessed the hearts of his own people, when diabolical forces turned the cross into a swastika and atheism became the religion of nations, our Lover leapt over the hills of human cruelty, the mountains of pride and indifference, to assure his faithful, to comfort them, to lead them ever toward a Promised Land.

Unfortunately, when the clouds seem to disperse, we settle for so little—little hills, little hoards of treasure, little collections of this world's goods—and this we do for the façade of self-importance. We surround ourselves with these hills. Hark, my Lover. Here he comes. He bounds over all these. He comes into my life. My hills crumble like the walls of Jericho (Joshua 6:20). They are no longer a strong defense, protecting a very fragile ego, a false self.

Am I willing to stand naked before my Lover? Will I seek to hide behind yet other walls? Or will I welcome him? Do I need to claim doings and rewards? Or can I accept a love that is totally gratuitous and therefore totally humbling?

How I fear defenselessness, even in the face of Love. Does his eagerness frighten me? Do I fear that such a Lover will demand all? He will!

How eager is the Love that is stopped by nothing. Loving, even as he mounts the Hill of Calvary. The lack of faith in his Chosen Ones seems to mark a total defeat. On the other side, only a tomb. But, hark, my Lover. Here he comes, leaping out of Sheol, the realm of the dead, bounding out of the Tomb. Be not unbelieving but believing.

Look again at our drawing. Let something of the almost wild enthusiasm of the Divine Lover touch your soul. No matter how rugged and piercing the peaks, no matter how dark and fearsome the lowering clouds, he comes. And nothing stops him! The Gospel according to St. Mark tells us Jesus was "distressed," "amazed" at the little faith he found among his own kin (Mark 6:6). Does this Divine Lover find more among us? Do we ever begin to allow the reality of such love to come in? It is what we most want, what we most deeply long for—to be loved by an insatiable, totally appreciative love.

We are made in God's image (Genesis 1:27), but we do not always act that way. We are God's Chosen People (John 15:16), but we do not always act that way. We are God's Beloved (Romans 9:25), but we do not always act that way. We must not allow our shame and guilt, our many repeated failures to lead us into denying who we are. Though our sins be as great as sharp peaks that pierce the sky, though our failures be as dark as the clouds of a stormy night, they do not change who we are. Nor do they impede our most zealous Lover. The only thing that can impede our Lover is ourselves. If we close our eyes and refuse to see, close our ears and refuse to hear, he cannot enter in. "Faith comes from hearing" (Romans 10:17). And this wondrous relation of love is a relation in faith, a relationship in which we believe in each other's love and trust in it: believe in his abounding and bounding love for us and our own love for him.

Do we love him, this Divine Lover? Really love him? This is what the Song of Songs is all about: an opportunity to discover the reality and depths of our own love in the face of such an insatiable Love. He leaps over the mountains, bounds over the hills only that he might call us forth to the love for which we were made and the love that alone can satisfy our being.

The Invitation

My Lover is like a gazelle or like a young stag.
There he stands behind our wall, gazing through the windows,
peering through the lattice.
My Loved One speaks to me,
"Arise, my Beloved, my Beautiful One, and come!
For now the winter is past, the rains are over and gone."

—*Song of Songs 2:9–11*

But there is one thing to which you must give complete attention:
that you always open wide your windows and lattices by your confes-
sions. Through these openings his kindly gaze can penetrate to our
inner life.... There are two kinds of confession—the one, sorrow for
our transgressions; the other, rejoicing for God's gifts. As often as I
make that confession of my sins which is accompanied by anguish of
heart, I open a lattice or a narrow window. I do not doubt but that
the devoted Examiner who stands behind the wall looks through it
with pleasure, because God will not despise a humble and contrite
heart (Psalm 50:19). We are even exhorted to this: Confess your iniq-
uities that you may be made righteous (Isaiah 43:26). But if at times,
when my heart expands in love at the thought of God's graciousness
and mercy, I rightly surrender my mind, to let it go in songs of praise
and gratitude, I feel that I have opened up to the Bridegroom who
stands behind the wall not a narrow lattice but a wide-open window.
Through it, unless I am mistaken, he will look with pleasure, the
greater the more he is honored by this sacrifice of praise.

—Bernard of Clairvaux, *Sermons on the Song of Songs*, 56:78

"My Lover is like a gazelle or like a young stag.
There he stands behind our wall,
gazing through the windows,
peering through the lattices."

דּוֹמֶה דוֹדִי לִצְבִי
אוֹ לְעֹפֶר הָאַיָּלִים
הִנֵּה־זֶה עוֹמֵד
אַחַר כָּתְלֵנוּ
מַשְׁגִּיחַ מִן־
הַחֲלֹנוֹת
מֵצִיץ מִן־
הַחֲרַכִּים

My beloved is like a gazelle
or like a young stag.
There he stands behind
our wall.
GAZING THROUGH THE WINDOW
Peering through the
Lattice   2:9

phillip ratner

The Invitation

*T*his Lover of ours: all the tenderness of the most graceful gazelle, yet all the majestic strength of the mighty stag are his. He comes to us with the greatest desire and longing. But he does not batter down the wall of faith.

This wall of faith, it has its windows and lattices. We see only through a glass, darkly (1 Corinthians 13:11). Each sighting has its own glass, its own degree of transparency, its own coloring. Unless we throw the windows completely open, the lattices are better. Yet in their narrowness they allow but glimpses, glimpses of the Divine through the bones, marrow, and sinews of the humanity of the Son of Man. Yet there can be a touch, a real touching. "He is the one we have touched" (1 John 1:1).

He comes. He entices. Yet, he ever respects our space. He stands behind the wall, yet uses all the openings to call us forth: a sight, a light, a touch, an odor of sweetness. How hard it is to believe that the Lover eagerly peers in, gazes upon us with love, that we are of such interest to this Divine Being, the delight of his eyes. The watchful intent of the Ever-Vigilant is upon us. His is a visage suffused with love, love for us.

Let us have the courage to come out from behind our walls, our defensiveness, to believe in this love, to be open and vulnerable to all the ravishments of Divine Love.

Like Moses, I cry out: "Show me yourself" (Exodus 33). Hide no longer behind the wall. Come through the windows of my soul. Break open the lattices and come in. Is it not you yourself who has come eagerly across mountains and hills to be with me? Certainly you did not come to remain behind a wall. I want kisses; I want the embrace that will make us one and fruitful.

But with Moses I hear, "One shall not see me and live" (Exodus 33:20). I do not want to live without you. I cannot live without you. Open the windows. Break open the lattices. And come in. Or else, "with my God, I will leap over the wall" (Psalm 18:30). I will break forth from all the restraints of this life, of this mortal body. I will go out of myself in ecstatic fervor and be I know not where—but no longer enclosed in the walls of this life—albeit but for an ecstatic moment. Is this not for what you have come: that your glance, filtered though it be by the glass of my faith, may yet pierce my being? Does not the opening of the lattices allow you to touch me with your word, which cuts to the marrow of my soul like a two-edged sword (Hebrews 4:12), cleaving its way to my inmost being, claiming all as your own?

Is it my sin, my indifference, my sluggishness that sets up this barrier? (Isaiah 59:2). But there are windows. You can look in and with your painful, healing glance call forth from my soul true repentance, as you did with sinful Peter (Luke 22:60). More, in your mercy and goodness, you can pass through the wall as you did on the day of your resurrection (John 20:19) and bring joy and new life to my wavering faith. By looking upon me you enable me to see you with renewed eyes of faith, and with renewed fervor my whole being longs to respond to your call of love: "Arise, my beloved, my beautiful one, and come!"

Oh, I would arise—rise above all that holds me back, all that separates us, all that obscures my vision of you. Help me to truly believe that I am your Beloved, that I am beautiful to you. Then I will dare to come and look in your eyes and see my true beauty in the creating power of your most merciful love. For it is your mercy that looks upon misery and makes it truly lovable. Yes, I will come in faith and hope so that I might be transformed in your love. May nothing hold me back. Open wide, you windows; expand, you lattices; fall to the ground, you walls. Let nothing stand between my Lover and me. I forsake all my defenses. I stand ready to be ravished by your love, by Love himself, cost what it may.

I am humbled, indeed, in the presence of this Lover. All the might of the haughty stag is his—and more: all the gracefulness of the sleek gazelle. He could easily knock down any wall. He could easily slip through any lattice. But to what purpose? Well he knows that if he but showed the least fringe of his glorious being, we, his Beloved, would be driven to stupefaction. His stunning beauty would stun us to totally engrossed awe. There would be no space for the freedom of love.

And so the Divine Lover, even with his awesome might and beauty, is reduced to being a beggar, begging for our love. "Behold, I stand at the door and knock and if one opens"—the great "if"—"I will come in and we will sit down side by side and sup together" (Revelation 3:20). This is the kind of loving intimacy that this Lover wants: two most intimate friends, breaking bread together. And not sitting across from each other but side by side, so that the Beloved can rest her head upon her Lover's bosom (John 13:23) and hear the beating of his most loving heart. It is the intimacy of the Eucharist, so hidden in sacramental veils yet allowing a communion of lovers that is beyond anything the human imagination could ever have conceived. These are the windows, these are the lattices: the inspired Scriptures, all of which have been written for our instruction (2 Timothy 3:16), and the Sacrament of Love himself. They give voice to the Lover. They bestir us: "Arise, make haste, my Beloved, my Beautiful One, and come!"

The Springtime of Love

The blossoms have appeared in the land, the time of pruning has
    come,
and the song of the turtledove is heard in our land.
The fig tree puts forth its figs, and the vines in flower give forth
    their sweet smell.
Arise, my Beloved, my Beautiful One, and come!
O my dove in the clefts of the rock, in the secret recesses of the cliff,
show me your face, let your voice sound in my ear,
for your voice is sweet and your face is lovely.
Catch us the foxes, the little foxes, that ruin the vineyards—
for our vineyards are in blossom.
My Loved One is mine and I am his; he pastures among the lilies.
Until the day breaks and the shadows flee,
return, my Loved One, be like a gazelle or a young stag up on the
    mountains of Bether.

—Song of Songs 2:12–17

"The blossoms have appeared in the land,
the time of pruning has come,
and the song of the turtledove is heard in our land."

הַנִּצָּנִים נִרְאוּ
בָאָרֶץ עֵת
הַזָּמִיר הִגִּיעַ
וְקוֹל הַתּוֹר
נִשְׁמַע בְּאַרְצֵנוּ

The blossoms have appeared
in the land,
The time of pruning has come;
The song of the turtledove
Is heard in our land. 2:12

philip ratner

The Springtime of Love

*H*ow mysterious, how mysterious are the ways of love.
Just when creation is its most glorious—full of life,
color, and fragrance—and all is uplifting, it is time for the savage shears of the pruner to come into play. But love will still
have its way. In the midst of it all, the uplifting song of the bird
of paradise, the dove—gentle, beckoning, intimate—is heard
even as it wings its way toward the heights, inviting us to ever
higher realms, to hidden heights.

It hasn't all happened in an instant. The passage or this call
to the higher realms has been demanding. The seed had to be
planted; it had to fall into the darkness of the earth and as it
were die (John 12:24). All the attachments, all the clinging loves
that held us too close to the earth: of all of these we had to let
go. We had to pass through a time of darkness, a seeming death,
so that new life could spring forth from the depths of our
being, from the deepest center where the Divine Creative
Energies ever bring us forth. With what patience we had to
abide the slow, slow process of growth. Through patience we
share in the passion of Christ; its life-giving vitality flows into
our being. There were the thorns all about and so many other
challenges to our growth (Matthew 13). But at last, at last, "the
blossoms have appeared in our land." Buds come forth, hope
grows. And finally the splendor of full blooms. With a beauty
beyond all our hopes and expectations—"not even Solomon in
all his glory was clothed as one of these" (Matthew 6:29)—not
only did we delight our Source of Life, our Divine Lover, but
our scent went forth, filling the whole house (John 12:3), enticing all about us to embrace the way of love.

For us there is not only delight in this moment of heady

perfumes and radiant blossoms. It all calls forth a hope of abundant fruitfulness. Why, then, why these brutal pruning shears? It is often so hard to understand why, after years of faithfulness, of great patience, just when our life seems to have blossomed and there is the expectation of great fruitfulness, all is suddenly threatened. Or worse, savagely cut away.

I cannot but help think of the stories of so many of the saints, like Francis of Assisi. At the very time their life had blossomed so fully and it seemed they should be celebrated and allowed to celebrate what had been accomplished, they were rejected and set aside by those whom they most loved and best served. But were they not, and are not we, disciples of the Lover who was betrayed by one of his dearest while the others fled? Was it not after years of bringing a word of life to the multitudes: "No man ever spoke like this man" (John 7:46) and healing every sort of ill—"Tell what you have seen and heard: the blind see again, the lame walk, lepers are cleansed, and deaf hear" (Luke 7:22)—that his life was cut down? No pruning shears were ever so brutal as the scourges that tore his back (John 19:1), as the derision that cut through his soul.

The Dove was the sacrament that descended from heaven at the moment of his baptism, the inauguration of his active ministry. The Dove is the manifestation of the Spirit of God. If we do not let ourselves become wholly absorbed in the hour of our pruning, whatever form it may take, we can still hear her sing. The call is still there: "Arise, make haste, my Beloved, my Beautiful One, and come!" (Song 2:13). But it is now a call to new, unseen heights. Yes, he allows the brutal pruning but he is still enamored: "Let me see you, let me hear your voice, for your voice is sweet, and you are lovely" (Song 2:4).

There are foxes hidden among our blossoms: little foxes, but capable of great damage. The Lover will pasture only among the purest of blossoms. Every invidious little movement of pride, self-centeredness, vanity, jealousy, envy—all of them must be cut away. Alas, we usually have to be brought very low, cut even to the root, totally exposed, before we finally are rid of all this. Then we can blossom as the purest of lilies and be the delightful place where the Divine Lover will love to pasture until the dawn of the eternal day. "Return, my Loved One, be like a gazelle" (Song 2:17). Yes, he will eagerly return and abide with us in the most gentle yet lofty of embraces.

Let us listen to the most inviting voice of the turtledove. It invites us to take flight as a dove, to fly on the wings of spiritual understanding, to fly away and enter the clefts of the rock who is our God (Psalm 18:2), to know and be known in the intimacy of a love beyond all telling. With passionate haste let us rise above all earthly things and come to him who restores our beauty. The storms of temptation are past; disorders that cooled and even at times froze our hearts are behind us now. We are now in the season of life when virtue can blossom. The virtues of this earthly garden can be many and varied, very beautiful and truly attractive. But the turtledove sings of something yet much higher. If we are but willing to be cut free from even the most beautiful things of creation, we can take wing and find that sacred cave where we can finally hear the still small voice that caused holy Elijah to cover his face (1 Kings 19:13).

In the Chamber

*U*pon my bed at night I sought him whom my soul loves;
I sought him, but found him not.
I will rise now and go about the city, in the streets and in the
squares;
I will seek him whom my soul loves.
I sought him, but found him not.
The watchmen found me, as they went about the city.
"Have you seen him whom my soul loves?"
Scarcely had I passed them, when I found him whom my soul loves.
I held him and would not let him go until I brought him into my
mother's house,
and into the room of her that conceived me.
I adjure you, Daughters of Jerusalem, by the gazelles or the does of
the fields:
do not arouse, do not awaken love until it pleases!

—Song of Songs 3:1–5

In the Chamber

(Gilbert of Hoyland, *Sermons on the Song of Songs*, 11:1–5)

*T*he affection of love is a delicate plant, and spiritual joy is wounded by the slightest mishap. Love frets over outward occupations, considering it enough to mind its own business. Love rejoices in leisure and is encouraged by repose. Love longs to have periods free for interior delights. Do you not think the bride implies this, when she draws her Loved One into the privacy of the chamber? She knows that, outside, her Loved One cannot be securely or even wholly possessed.... How hard it is, I say, to admit alien cares to the rights of perfect love and to disturb the heavenly mystery with throngs of worldlings. "I was mindful of God," says the Psalmist, "and I was delighted, but I was drained and my spirit grew faint" (Psalm 76:4). If delight drains itself and exhausts the Prophet's spirit in the business of remembering God, how can many and alien affairs be embraced along with God? Rightly then does the Bride seek the chamber with her Loved One that she may wait upon him with unhampered attention, enjoy him with freedom of spirit, and embrace him utterly with peace of heart. Clearly she who seeks in this way an opportunity of engaging in love is led by the spirit of charity and has spoken with the affection of a bride....

The inestimable beauty of the Divine Majesty, once revealed, commends itself to pure minds, ravishes the affection of the beholder, and in some way makes the mind like itself, allowing it to think of nothing else. We are lured by scent, but we are transformed by sight. Good then is the practice of contemplation, which confers upon the human mind a common

outlook and brings it into conformity with the supreme
Majesty. Good it is to dwell here, for desires lure us no further,
and desires should not stop our advancing so far. Who will
grant that this may be my rest forever and ever? Happy the one
who can say from his heart: "This is my dwelling, for I have
chosen it" (Psalm 131:14). Mary has chosen the best part,
which shall not be taken away from her (Luke 10:42).
Knowledge will pass, prophecies will disappear, tongues will
cease (1 Corinthians 13:8); contemplation alone will not fail in
the future. Therefore choose this part for yourself for the present, for this part will never be taken away, that your soul may
say: "The Lord is my part" and therefore I shall contemplate
him. The Prophet says: "Therefore I shall look for him"
(Lamentations 3:24). And rightly, because he looks for the fullness of goodness, a portion of which he already possesses. One
who here enjoys the good of contemplation may look for
something more of the same kind, but ought not to look for
something different.

These good things are blessings stored up for many years
(Luke 12:19), indeed for years without end. Happy then are
you, O Soul, if you enjoy this good; dine, feast, for your portion will not be taken away, but will be more bountifully
renewed and reformed. This is your rest forever and ever.
"This is my dwelling, for I have chosen it" (Psalm 131:14).
Dwell here, that you may dwell with him who sits above the
Cherubim (Isaiah 37:16), above the fullness of knowledge,
who "dwells in light inaccessible" (1 Timothy 6:16). So let your
place be in the light of contemplation. This is the proper and
familiar place of your mother the Church, this is her house;
other duties, which she carries out to meet temporal needs,
look to this end. Duties of the active life are transient; those of
the contemplative life are permanent. It is good for you to be
here; here build a tabernacle for yourself, not one for yourself

and another for your Loved One but one for the two of you (Matthew 17:4).

Introduce your Loved One into this chamber. Enter into your repose that you may rest from your labors, as God did from his. On the seventh day he rested from the work of creation (Genesis 2:2); on the seventh day he rested from the work of restoration (Luke 23:56). On the former day, after he established the universe; on the latter, when he hid himself in the tomb. On the former day, after setting the universe on its foundation; on the latter, after renewing mankind. If you have sought, if you have found, if you have taken hold of your Loved One, hold fast the one you hold. Hold fast, cling to him, press yourself upon him, that his image, expressed as it were in you, may be renewed, that you may be the imprint of his seal. But this you will be, if you cling to him, "for the one who clings to God is one spirit with God" (1 Corinthians 6:17). Perhaps it is difficult at first to imprint him upon yourself as upon hard metal. But if the imprinting is laborious, the clinging is sweet. Laborious is the sixth day of your reformation, but sweet are the Sabbaths of rest that follow....

Because of the Sabbath after the creation, when the new man had been created on the sixth day, one is told that God rested from his works on the seventh (Genesis 2:2). Do you also secure a Sabbath for yourself; redeem your time (Ephesians 5:15), and claim hours free from outward occupation.

But take care lest enemies mock your Sabbaths, lest your times of leisure serve them, lest you be free for them, when you should have been free for God. "Be free and see that I am God," says the Psalmist (Psalm 45:11). Leisure is good, but "write of wisdom in your time to leisure" (Sirach 38:25). Write wisdom on the breadth of your heart. For the heart is broad which is not shriveled by cares. Imprint in the depth of your heart letters which are indelible, and inscribe characters of wisdom on the tablets of your spirit, that you may be able to say: "The light of your countenance was stamped upon us, O Lord; you have put gladness into my heart" (Psalm 4:7). Rejoice and keep holiday with your Loved One, feasting, as it is written, at the entrance of such glory (Psalm 75:11). "The Sabbath," as Isaiah says, "is the delightful and holy and glorious day of the Lord" (Isaiah 58:13). "Delightful and holy," he says.... If you are free, you have a Sabbath; if you are free and have eyes to contemplate the delights of the Lord, then your Sabbath is "delightful and holy," a glorious Sabbath of the Lord; a Sabbath within a Sabbath, that is freedom in freedom.

The first freedom is good, if you are not free for the world. The second indeed is better, if you are free for yourself and think of how you may please God (1 Corinthians 7:32). The third is the best, if, forgetful even of yourself, you are free only for God and think of what concerns the Lord, how he may be pleasing to you. Let not your Sabbath be one of idleness; perform the work of God on your Sabbath. Now the work of God is that you should believe in him. It is by faith that you see. Indeed we see now in a mirror (1 Corinthians 13:12); therefore be free, that you may see. Sight, and especially the sight of God, is a delightful work.

The King upon His Couch

What is this coming up from the desert,
like a column of aromatic smoke, myrrh, frankincense,
and every powder of the perfumer?
Look, there is Solomon's couch
encircled by sixty warriors, of the warriors of Israel,
all of them with swords, men most skilled in battle,
each with his sword at his side against the terrors of the night.
King Solomon made himself a palanquin of timber from Lebanon.
He made its poles of silver, its canopy of gold, its cushions of
    purple,
its interior fitted out with love for the Daughters of Jerusalem.

—Song of Songs 3:6–10

*"There is Solomon's couch
encircled by sixty warriors, of the warriors of Israel."*

הִנֵּה מִטָּתוֹ שֶׁלִּשְׁלֹמֹה שִׁשִּׁים גִּבֹּרִים סָבִיב לָהּ מִגִּבֹּרֵי יִשְׂרָאֵל

There is solomons Couch,
Encircled by sixty warriors
Of the warriors of ISRAEL.....
3:7

The King upon His Couch

*L*ove knows nothing of fear, even of honor, only closeness, intimacy, and embrace. It rejoices that the Lover is exalted, King of kings, Lord of lords, the King of Peace, the true Solomon. The Beloved can only be filled with joy at seeing her Loved One make his grand entry. She can only be incited the more when she sees him arrive in regal splendor, the rich cortege surrounded and totally embraced by sweet-smelling clouds of the choicest incense. Anything other than an audacious love would draw back and fear to approach such an exalted one. But this reverential distancing is certainly not what the King of Love wants, nor the reason for his display of splendor.

The King of Love wants only that the Beloved give herself to him totally in a love that is complete and knows nothing but love. For this he comes, leaving behind him the barrenness of the desert, filling the air with enticements to love. And he will use his stoutest warriors, all the might of heaven and earth, to protect the domain of love, the primacy of their intimacy. Mary has chosen the best part, and it will not be taken away from her (Luke 10:42). So, too, for anyone else who audaciously chooses the part of contemplative intimacy.

For her part, the Beloved, the faithful one, like valiant Judith, must be willing to go out from the safety of the familiar, from the demanding embrace of family and friends (Judith 10:10), and pass through the phalanx that guards the secrets of the King in order to approach his very couch. She must forget her father's house (Psalm 45:10); she must let go of any clinging love, any possessiveness, any effort to create a false self by what she has, what she does, what others think of her. But this is not abandonment of them; it is not a lack of caring love. The Lord tears all our possessive loves out of our hearts only to hurl those loved back in, to be held with an infinite caring love. One with the Lover, the Beloved shares totally his caring, infinitely compassionate love for all who are the King's— the whole human family. With the self-giving love that led the King, thorn-crowned, to ascend the throne of the cross on Calvary's Hill, the true Beloved of the King of Peace is with him an agent of reconciliation, seeking to make all one in the communion of love.

If those who surround the couch of the King are warriors, they are there to preserve the tranquility of order that is peace, not only within the bowers of contemplation but in all the affairs of life. For Solomon, the King of Peace, wishes to share his peace with all the sons and daughters of the Kingdom.

When the King of Peace abides with us and his holy angels surround us, we no longer need in any way fear the powers of darkness. Again and again he showed his power to cast out demons (Mark 1:27, 34). In face-to-face combat before he left the desert he bested their leader (Luke 4:2–13). He has given his angels charge over us lest in the darkness we be led astray or molested in any way (Psalm 91:11).

If Solomon's retinue are mighty men who bear swords in order to strike fear in the agents of darkness, the reason he wears a radiant crown on his palanquin is in no way to inspire fear. It is to encourage hope. All his might, all his authority is at the disposal of the Beloved. The curtains are drawn back and raised high to allow all the desire of the King to shine forth. He comes, not only as a vision of enticing beauty, surrounded by all that is beautiful: silver and gold, royal purple, and intricate inlays. He reaches out with the sweetest of scents, which intoxicate the Beloved, drawing her into the ecstasy of love.

When the Lover comes to us thus, there is nothing for us

but to audaciously press forward and find our place upon the royal couch, to rest with him in the intimacy of contemplation.

What is this crown our King wears so proudly—this crown given him by his mother on the day of his wedding? Is it not his humanity, the crown of creation, which Mary gave the Son of God on the day he wed his People, becoming one with them? To be human is a glorious thing. Compared to divinity it may seem like nothing. All too often in our idolatry, making ourselves our own god, we do not appreciate the wonderful gift of humanity. True, the crown does not make the King. The glory of Christ's divinity may make his crown of humanity seem like a mere ornament. But he who made it knows its unique value and holds it most precious and wears it gloriously even in his triumph as he sits on his exalted throne—but only after wearing it in complete solidarity with us, his Beloved, whom he came to win to himself, becoming like us in all but sin (Philippians 2:7). If the crown of his humanity now shines with such luster it is because it was well polished by all the cares of everyday life, by a constant labor of love, by a total sacrifice of self. His crown, however especially lustrous it is by reason of his great love, is far from something that would elevate him above us; it is rather an expression of his total solidarity with us. It bespeaks one who understands with complete compassion all we struggle with, all we suffer, because he himself has taken on and lived our human life.

Having won the victory over death and the grave, he will wear his crowning humanity as a glorious trophy even when he comes to us in glory, surrounded by his mighty army of angels. He will come surrounded by the sweet odor of all his saints and holy ones. He will come with the perfume of his own glorious triumph. He comes to celebrate an eternal nuptial with his People. To each of the faithful comes the awesome invitation to join him in the most intimate of embraces upon his palanquin of glory, that with him we might be escorted into heavenly glory.

Behold our Solomon, sitting on his palanquin, adorned with the crown he was crowned with on the day of his wedding with his People.

A Crowned Lover

O maidens of Zion, go forth and gaze upon King Solomon wearing the crown that his mother gave him on his wedding day, on his day of bliss.

—*Song of Songs 3:11*

*H*ow you ought to have rejoiced over such a wedding, faithful soul! How you ought to have rejoiced and kept high holiday! (Psalm 75:11) Dress up, dress up in the robes of your glory, holy city (Isaiah 52:4), bride of the Lamb; rejoice and be glad, O Zion united to Christ! How will you not rejoice while he himself rejoices? "The Bridegroom will rejoice over the bride," says Isaiah, "and your God will rejoice over you" (Isaiah 62:5). But with how much joy? "On the day of his wedding," says the Song, "on the day of the bliss of his heart" (Song 3:11). No slight emotion of gladness was intended, for the text mentioned the joy of his heart. Do I say gladness? It is sheer delight. "My delights," we read in Proverbs, "are to be with the children of men" (Proverbs 8:31).... It is an insult to the Bridegroom, if while he rejoices you do not applaud from your heart, do not congratulate him, and fail to rejoice with him.

—Gilbert of Hoyland, *Sermons on the Song of Songs*, 20:9

*"O maidens of Zion, go forth and gaze
upon King Solomon
wearing the crown that his mother
gave him on his wedding day,
on his day of bliss."*

maidens of Zion, go forth And gaze upon King Solomon Wearing the crown that his mother GAVE him on his wedding day, On his day of Bliss.   3:11

A Crowned Lover

*B*lissful indeed for us is the day when the King of Peace, the Blessed Solomon, the eternal King, the true Lover becomes the Bridegroom of his People, inviting them into an intimacy that ever remains beyond anything they can conceive: "Eye has not seen, nor ear heard, nor has it entered into the human mind what God has prepared for those who love him" (1 Corinthians 2:9).

We hear in our times of the "universal call to holiness." Here it is indeed. Every maiden of Zion, every one of his People who has not wed herself to false gods, has not allowed other kings to rule her heart, is indeed invited to enjoy the gaze of contemplation. In fact, even those of us who have allowed ourselves to be wed to the false gods of this world, making alliance with power and pleasure and money and seeking to produce their fruits in our lives—yes, even we are invited to gaze upon our King and Savior. For nothing can more surely, effectively, and quickly turn us from the false gods than a perception, an experience of the true God, our true King, wherein we can find all joy and the steady and lasting fulfillment of all our deepest longings. The sight of our true King will dethrone all the other kings who have sought to rule over our hearts.

Maidens of Zion, Daughters of Jerusalem, flock around. Here is your King. There is no better rallying point. There is no more delightful sight. There is no greater unity than that which we find in him, our King and our God. We are his People, one People, a holy People, a priestly People, a People set apart (1 Peter 2:9). Go forth in virginal innocence, in the singlehearted-ness of a maidenhood totally centered on him. For this is what is necessary to see him: "Blessed, happy are the pure of heart"—true maidens—"for they shall see God" (Matthew 5:8). He has chosen us (John 15:16). It is for us to choose him.

Oh blissful day when he leapt down from the bosom of the Father to wed our humanity and received from Mary, the maiden mother (Isaiah 7:14), the crown of our humanity, becoming the Firstborn of all the sons and daughters of the Father.

We hear again Isaiah's words and wonder at them:

But you shall be called "My Delight,"
and your land "Espoused."
For the Lord delights in you,
And makes your land his spouse.
As a young man marries a virgin,
Your Lover shall marry you;
And as a Bridegroom rejoices in his Bride,
So shall your God rejoice in you.

—*Isaiah 62:4–5*

It is the day of the bliss of his heart.

How can it be? This God so lofty, so great, beyond all greatness—how should he take on our lowly humanity and take it on as a crown? True, humanity is the crown of his creation, but yet it is so lowly in comparison to its Creator. How can it be that he should delight in us his People? He has told us. We have adulterous hearts. We constantly go after false gods (Hosea 2): not now Aaron's golden calf (Exodus 32:4) or the demigods of Ba'al (1 Kings 18:19). But still, we all too easily make our own idols: a car, a house, a reputation, money in the bank. How can he take delight in us?

Yet, this is in fact the whole purpose of his creation: that he might have someone with whom he can share his joy. Joy needs to be shared. Love of its very nature needs someone to love, needs to be creative. He has gone so far as to make us in his own image (Genesis 1:27) so that he may share with us all that he is, all that he has. In those first days of creation his delight was to walk in the garden in the cool of the evening (Genesis 3:8), enjoying all with the couple he had made. This was his beautiful plan. And he will not be frustrated.

We have sinned. We know our sin and shame and would cover it ineffectively with something of our own craft, be it but an apron made of fig leaves (Genesis 3:7). But God quickly provided better and promised yet more (Genesis 3:15). The time of fulfillment has come. Our King has come to us. And he made the crown of his creation to be his crown. In this he has restored us. It is time to cast off all our shame and shamelessly go forth and gaze in contemplative wonder upon our glorious King. For with joy and gladness of heart he has received from that woman who is the glory of his creation, the holy Virgin Mary, the crown that makes him one with us and makes it possible for us to be one with him.

Let all of Zion—young men and maidens, old men and children, too (Psalm 148:2)—let all gather around and raise hands and hearts and captive eyes to behold this wondrous apparition of divine glory in the midst of his People. Well has the Wiseman declared, "The fascination of trifles obscures the good" (Wisdom 4:12). How easily we are fascinated by the passing baubles of his creation and fail to see how they all proclaim the goodness, munificence, and love of their Creator, how they all point to him. Indeed, how he is in them, every moment giving them the beauty, truth, and being they possess. Rightly we sing: Crown him with many crowns. All creation is meant to be his crown. Like a thousand lamps they are to reveal him in all his goodness and majesty. This is our King. Yes, ours. For all things are ours and we are his, even as he is God's (1 Corinthians 3:23).

Let us fix our eyes upon him. Let our weary wandering and

searching come to an end. May the sight of our King so crowned and crowning so captivate us that our gaze will never stray again to alien and passing attractions. Ever fixed on him, let us find in him the One who alone can truly fulfill all the aspirations of our being for infinite love, eternal life, joy, beauty, and peace.

We are all called. Indeed, it is more than a call. It is an imperious summons. For he is our King and we are his People (Psalm 100:3). He has every right to demand our attention. But this is the King of Love. If he calls, commands, it is only for our own joy and fulfillment. His is a true love: It seeks not its own (1 Corinthians 13:5). He seeks only to share joy, boundless joy. Let us gaze upon him. Gaze upon him, and we will want nothing more. Our restless hearts will at last find rest. The King of Peace, the true Solomon, will invade our hearts with his peace. We are summoned to the kingdom of peace. When all eyes rest on him there can only be universal and lasting peace. Then the wolf shall live with the lamb and the leopard lie down with the kid…no hurt, no harm will be done on his holy mountain (Isaiah 11:6–9).

The Beloved

Ah, you are fair, my darling.
Ah, you are fair with your dove-like eyes behind your veil.
Your hair is like a flock of goats streaming down the mountains of
    Gilead.
Your teeth are like the flock of shorn ewes,
which come up from the washing,
all of them big with twins, none of them barren.
Your lips a crimson ribbon and your voice, sweet.
Your cheek is like a half-pomegranate behind your veil.
Your neck is David's tower, girt with battlements;
A thousand shields hang upon it, all the equipment of valiant men.
Your breasts are like twin fawns, the young of a gazelle, among the
    lilies.
Till the day breaks and the shadows retire,
I will go to the mountain of myrrh and to the hill of frankincense.
You are all fair, my Beloved, and there is no blemish in you.
Come from Lebanon, my Bride, come from Lebanon,
come from the peak of Amana, from the peak of Senir and
    Hermon,
from the lions' haunts, from the mountains of the leopards.

—Song of Songs 4:1–8

"Ah, you are fair, my darling.
Ah, you are fair with your dove-like eyes."

הִנָּךְ יָפָה
רַעְיָתִי
הִנָּךְ יָפָה
עֵינַיִךְ
יוֹנִים׃

Ah, you are fair
my darling, Ah, you
are fair,
with your dove-like
eyes.

1:15

Philip Ratner

The Beloved

Ah, ah, ah.... Perhaps that is all that can be said, all that should be said. The whole of creation can but breathe forth an aspiration of admiring love and loving admiration in the presence of such loveliness. But that the Eternal, the Bridegroom, the Divine Lover should be reduced to gasps of love in the presence of one of his creation.... The Chosen has all too often prided itself on being the Chosen, but how difficult we find it to accept ourselves as lovers who with eyes of love can make the Divine Lover gasp: Ah, ah, ah....

But should not he who is love itself be most vulnerable to love, most appreciative of love, most susceptible to love? Whether the eyes of love be wide open, surrounded by the flutter of enticing lashes like the wings of fluttering doves, or demurely closed, veiling their majestic power, their penetrating rays of love wound, enthrall, draw together into one the Perceiver and the Perceived. The Beloved needs but to allow the inner fires of love to gently shine out these windows of the soul to wholly entrance the Lover. For he has made us for love, to find all our delight in loving Love and in being loved by the Divine Lover.

If we but dare to open our eyes and see ourselves in the eyes of the Lover, open our ears to his praise, we will come to know that we are indeed loved and lovable. No veil can hide such beauty from him as he reaches out for every simile to give some expression to it, all the exaggerations, all the fantasies of a Lover: You are all beautiful! There is no blemish in you.

As your radiant eyes gently close they draw within. All the beauty of the queen is within (Psalm 45:14). Is it not a beauty too great to be recorded, a beauty beyond human thought and expression? Pile up all your similes. Exaggerate all you will: dove-like eyes, long-haired goats, shorn ewes and twin fawns, David's tower, its shields and battlements. No words, no wonders of the creation of God or of humans can adequately express the true beauty of love. God is Love. It is love that is the truest expression of the Divine within us. In love, the image of God that we are most fully attains the Divine Likeness.

Well does the Beloved close her eyes and seek refuge behind her veil as the Lover pours out his praises. Open-eyed simplicity cannot deny the truth of what she hears from Truth and sees reflected in the eyes of Truth. Nevertheless, there is a due shyness, if not shame. For all our beauty is but a reflection of his, his creation, created to give him delight. "Not unto us, O Lord, not unto us, but unto your Name give the glory" (Psalm 115:1). So loving is the Lover that he finds his delight only in sharing his love, a love that delights in love and in calling forth love, and in a mercy that is greater than love. For love responds to the good and the beautiful, but mercy responds to misery and makes it lovable, imparting to it goodness and beauty.

Well might cheeks flame like ruddy pomegranates, whose veiled presence cannot be hidden. What can one expect from a sinner but sin! Yet, here is an undeniable beauty that claims the loving admiration of even a God. What lavish mercy has bestowed all this? It demands the deepest humility; it takes the greatest simplicity, the simplicity of the dove (Matthew 10:16) to acknowledge it, to accept the work of love in us and to accept the love that the product of that love evokes.

How can such a love yet be so gentle with the gentleness of the dove? It is the mysterious enchantment of pools that hide in the greatest depths their mysterious allure. Simplicity allows no cloudiness of mixed intent to obscure the radiant darkness that beckons. All awaits the infusion of the Divine Light that can accept no admixture. It is only the pure of heart who can see the true God of love (Matthew 5:8). All others accept lesser gods whom they hope to tame and use. But they are destined to be frustrated like the priests of Ba'al and go to their deaths while Divine Fire enlightens the People of God and confirms the true Messenger, who brings the message of a Divine Lover who is ever faithful to covenanted love (1 Kings 18).

Hers is a ravishing beauty, a strong beauty, a fruitful beauty, this beauty of the Beloved. Though it is a beauty that has been praised in similes so rich they exhaust the human imagination, yet it is a beauty that evokes an enticing invitation to leave off all haughtiness, to come down from the heights that would pretend or need to pretend to any beauty of their own. It is an invitation to leave behind all our natural and savage ways that make us kin to lions and leopards. We can come from the far-off land, the Lebanon of unlikeness. The beauty of simplicity, sincerity, and truth, the purity and sweetness and strength with which we have been graced, makes us worthy even to enter into the Promised Land, the Lover's garden of delights. Yes, even to hear and respond to his pressing invitation to share his gorgeous bower and experience his intimate love.

True, till the eternal day of Resurrection breaks we must find our Loved One on the mount of myrrh, Calvary's Hill, in the shadow of the cross. Great though our love may be, enticing be the moments of contemplation, fragrant though the hill has become with its evening sacrifice—an incense that burned with love even as the powers of darkness sought to convulse the earth—we must be content with far less than what will satisfy us. We can see but the back of the swiftly passing Lord (Exodus 33:23) until the coming of the new heaven and new earth (Revelation 21:1), where the Divine Love is established as the Light therein (Revelation 21:23).

A Source of Delight

You have ravished my heart, my Sister, my Bride;
you have ravished my heart with one glance of your eyes,
with one hair on your neck.
How beautiful are your breasts, my Sister, my Bride;
how much more delightful are your breasts than wine
and the fragrance of your ointments than all spices!
Sweetness drips from your lips, O Bride;
honey and milk are under your tongue,
and the scent of your robes is like the scent of Lebanon.
You are an enclosed garden, my Sister, my Bride,
an enclosed garden, a fountain sealed.
You are a park that puts forth pomegranates
with all choice fruits, with henna, with spikenard,
with nard and saffron, calamus and cinnamon, with all the trees of
    Lebanon,
with myrrh and aloes and all the finest spices.
You are a garden fountain, a well of living water,
flowing fresh from Lebanon.

—Song of Songs 4:9–15

"Sweetness drips from your lips, O Bride;
honey and milk are under your tongue,
and the scent of your robes is like the scent of Lebanon."

נפת תטפנה שפתותיד כלה
דבש וחלב תחת לשונך וריח
שלמתיד כריח לבנון

Sweetness drops from your lips O bride;
Honey and milk are under your tongue;
And the scent of your robes
Is like the scent of Lebanon.
4:11

A Source of Delight

*T*hose dove-like eyes have done their work. Their least glance has ravished and calls forth an overflowing effusion of praise. Love does not need to speak with logic. Indeed, it cannot; far too cramping are the confines of the logical mind. Only imagery, poetry, and imagination can begin to give anything like satisfying expression to the passions of the heart. If we are not poets we can only stammer. If we are poets we pour out such a profusion of words and images that we but invite others into our addled mind. Who—what can express what needs to be said if we begin to speak of what totally ensnares our hearts?

There are the eyes, the windows of the soul. If all the queenly beauty is hidden within (Psalm 45:14), it cannot long be hidden when these windows dare to open to the Loved One. Her beauty everywhere makes itself present like the fragrance of the choicest ointments. A seemingly stray hair invites to the exquisite beauty of the most gracious neck. Breasts, full and round, are intoxicating like a strong wine.

But it is to the lips that the Lover's lips would rush. Lips seek lips. No words are needed here. Lips touch lips and only sweetness, a sweetness that flows through all one's being. A nourishing sweetness as tongue breaks through and tastes the delights within: milk, the lispings of needy prayer from babes, nourishing milk, and honey that carries the more experienced to yet greater heights of sweetest delight.

All is enwrapped in the sweet odor of cedar, the choicest scent from Lebanon hills. May it so enwrap us that the ecstasy of sweetness will last forever, no sublime burial box but a chamber of eternal love.

The Lover is to us as we need: milk to nourish when we are yet weak (1 Corinthians 3:1–2). Too much sweetness too soon can break the spirit. But sweetness there is—and ever more: sights and savors and scents that belie all of which we can speak. All the fragrance of the East, the richest of spices: What are these, overwhelming though they are, compared with that which inundates us when the Kiss is granted and we are drawn within? He purified Isaiah's lips with a burning coal (Isaiah 6:6–7). With his hand he touched Jeremiah's (Jeremiah 1:9). But this is hardly what we want or desire. Kiss me with the kisses of your lips. We want nothing less.

The invitations of the Lover may seem wounding. They seem to threaten our very being. Will there be anything left of us if we allow their blandishments full sway? But wait. It is the Lover who speaks here of his Beloved, a lowly one. Does the Divine Lover really find so much in us? Yes, he would have it so: "I no longer call you servants but friends. I convey to you all that the Source of All conveys to me" (John 15:15). Lovers share everything. "How sweet are your words to my taste, sweeter than honey in my mouth" (Psalm 119:103). All the abundant sweetness of the Divine Lover is ours. And is ours so that in turn we can attract and delight our Divine Lover, even as we find our all in him. He savors the sweetness of our lips as from our tongue come words of love and praise, a stream of sweetness that delights him. He finds nourishment and sweetness under our tongue when we welcome him in Holy Communion. In turn, when we open to the Lover the depths that are closed to all others, torrents of sweetness flow into us from the abundance of his sweetness. We experience the intoxicating richness of our being as it bears abundant fruit, watering this world with saving grace.

We are a garden of delights because we share all that our Lover is to God and God's creation. Let us open our lips that he may come in; then we will raise our head high in ecstasy: My God, I thank you for the wonder of my being (Psalm 139:14). The overflowing sweetness of our being will billow behind in voluminous robes, a wondrous presence and deeds that sweeten the lives of all who are graced to come near.

Let us fear not to abandon ourselves to the Divine blandishments, to give ourselves to the kiss of contemplation. Our Divine Lover will fill us, will share with us his all, and the fullness will overflow to give delight to all the City of God, to all the People of God. Even as we seem to abandon them and become a garden enclosed, our fruitfulness will abound to the delight and benefit of all. Our fountain may seem sealed as we no longer busy ourselves about many things (Luke 10:14), but our lives will give forth a sweet odor that will fill the whole house (John 12:3), making life more beautiful for the whole Church, for all the People of God. We will indeed be a garden fountain, a source of living water.

Yes, our Lover will kiss us with the Kiss of his mouth and find in us milk and honey, all that will give him delight.

My Garden

Awake, O north wind; come, O south wind,
blow upon my garden that its perfume may spread.
Let my Loved One come to his garden
and enjoy its luscious fruits.
I come to my garden, my Sister, my Bride;
I gather my myrrh with my spice,
I eat my honeycomb with my honey,
I drink my wine with my milk.
Eat, Friends, drink,
and be drunk with love.

—Song of Songs 4:16–5:1

"Awake, O north wind; come, O south wind,
blow upon my garden that its perfume may spread.
Let my Loved One come to his garden
and enjoy its luscious fruits."

עורי צפון ובואי תימן הפיחי גני יזלו בשמי יבא דודי

מגנו ויאכל פרי

Awake, O North Wind Come O south wind! Blow upon my garden, that its perfume may spread. Let my beloved come to his garden And enjoy its Lucious FRUITS! 4:16

My Garden

*T*his beautiful and enticing song of the Bride gives witness to the fact that the Beloved has come to make her
own two very significant insights.

The first is complete openness to life. We welcome, indeed,
the winds from the south. They bring to an end the frigid cold
from the north. Their warmth calls forth our gardens, fills
them with new life, brings out fragrant blossoms of all colors
and scents, gives promise to the rich harvest that is to come.
When the south winds come we are filled with new joy and
hope. However, the Bride in her maturity of spirit now wel-
comes not only the balmy, gentle, warming breezes from the
south but also the harsh, frigid, chilling blasts from the north.
She has come to know by the dark nights, by the seeming fruit-
less and perilous searches amidst the dangers of the city, by dis-
appointments and delays, that there are in the virtuous life
certain perfumes that can be released only by undergoing these
painful moments in the search for God.

Patience has a perfect work, for through patience we share
in the Passion of Christ, the crowning event and expression of
love in the history of God's People. The sweet odor of this lavish pouring out not only filled the whole house (John 12:3); its
sweetness spread through the whole world (Isaiah 27:6,
Matthew 26:13, Colossians 1:6), uplifting the spirits of all who
perceived its saving scent.

Disappointment generously endured engenders detachment, a freedom to find serenity in the things we cannot
change and the courage to go forward and change the things we
can change. No longer does the Beloved stay locked in her
own small chamber, afraid of soiling her feet if she steps out in

pursuit of her Lover. His touches, even the gentlest and most quickly passing, fill her with a daring that lets a pungent myrrh lend its strong note to her potpourri of aromas. Fortitude and perseverance in the quest can only win out and attract the valiant spirit of her powerful Lover. Tears can wash even the most beautiful face and give it a new luster, a ruddiness that is enticing when these tears flow from eyes that sparkle with love. In the divine quest, tears of sorrow quickly turn into tears of joy when detachment has enabled the seeker to center on the Other rather than on self.

Both north wind and south wind release their own particular scents, blending them together into a life richly human, enticing the Divine. For the delight of God is the human person fully alive.

When all the virtues, those of the smile and those of the tears, give forth each its own very special odor and blend together to create their unsurpassable perfume, then indeed is the garden of the Beloved ready for the Loved One, to offer him the richest fare. What greater delight can the Beloved have than to behold the Lover in her garden eagerly gathering its fruits, enjoying each one, celebrating the fruitfulness of his Beloved.

But note, a transformation has taken place—an important and profound transformation. When the Bride summoned the winds, north and south, it was to her garden. But now that the winds have worked their wonders and brought forth and blended all the potential sweetness of this garden, a transformation has truly taken place. For the Bride with new insight it is no longer "my garden," but she beckons the Loved One to come to "his garden." For the winds that have come in response to the Bride's ardent prayer are the winds of the Spirit, the Holy Spirit of Love, who from the first day of creation hovered over the waters of the deep, breathing in the life that would make all not only evolve but increase and multiply (Genesis 1:2). It is the same Spirit who breathed upon the Church gathered fearfully in the Upper Room (Acts 2:2–6) and sent them forth to bring their message to all the earth (Psalm 48:10). It is the Spirit of Love who will make all one. By the wondrous workings of the Spirit's unitive love, responding to and flowing from an operative faith and a vibrant active hope, a divinization has been wrought in the Beloved. "I live, now not I, but Christ lives in me" (Galatians 2:20). God beholds in me his Beloved, with whom he is well pleased (Matthew 3:17). The attraction is compelling. When we say, "Let my Loved One come," he can only say: "I come. I come to my garden."

He comes to gather the sweetest of spices: love, joy, peace, patience, long-suffering, kindness, goodness, gentleness, self-control: all the fruits of the Spirit (Galatians 5:22): And he also gathers the myrrh, first offered to him by wise men from the east (Matthew 2:11) but which his own most faithful brought to him the night he completed his loving sacrifice (John 19:39). All we have suffered in our quest for him, to prepare ourselves for him to be worthy of him, is precious to him, a pungent perfume he would not be without. For he made it completely his own in his journey from Bethlehem to the summit of Calvary. He takes to himself, as it were a food totally assimilated, not only the sweetness that flows from our lives but even the very "comb" from which it flows. We are totally his. He drinks with us the intoxicating wine of ecstatic love and the nourishing milk of unlimited mercy. The banquet in "our garden," the restored Paradise whose gates have been thrown wide open, is rich and unending.

And it is not only with his Beloved, his Bride, that the Divine Lover wants to enjoys this bounty. He cries out to all his Friends, to all his Chosen People, to all the human family: Come and be fed. And more: Come and know the intoxication of love. Do not all his saints, those most beautiful of gardens, beginning with his own dearest Mother and down through the centuries to a Mother Teresa of Calcutta and a Reverend Martin Luther King, find the Loved One drawing his Friends into their gardens, there to care for them, inspire them, and challenge them to enter ever more fully into the exciting and fulfilling quest that is love?

The Dream Visit

I sleep, but my heart watches.
The voice of the Loved One is knocking.
"Open to me, my Sister, my Love, my Dove, my Immaculate One,
for my head is wet with dew, my locks with the drops of the night."
I have put off my garment; should I put it on again?
I have bathed my feet; should I soil them?
My Loved One thrust his hand through the opening,
and my inmost being trembled at his touch.
I arose to open to my Loved One.
My hands dripped with myrrh, my fingers with the choicest myrrh
upon the bolt of the door.
I opened for my Loved One, but he had turned and gone.
My soul melted when he spoke.
I sought him, but did not find him; I called him, but he gave no
    answer.
The sentinels who go about the city found me;
they beat me, they wounded me, they stripped me of my mantle,
those sentinels of the walls.
I adjure you, Daughters of Jerusalem,
if you find my Loved One, tell him I am faint with love.

—Song of Songs 5:2–8

The Dream Visit

(Gilbert of Hoyland, *Sermons on the Song of Songs*, 42:1–4)

*L*ove is utterly overwhelming in its power, bemusing the senses like the most potent wine. One only needs to listen to the description in the Song of Solomon to see how God's love inebriates and dazes the soul. "I lie asleep," says the Bride in the Song. We can imagine her saying to her Lover: "You invite me to drink deep of your love; how can I resist the grace you offer me? I lie asleep, but my heart is awake. I take my rest, laying aside all thought of daily tasks, and so give free rein to my heart, allowing it to revel in the intoxicating wine of your love."

What a wonderful sequence we have here! Intoxication leads to sleep, and sleep gives rise to watchfulness.

"I lie asleep, yes," continues the Bride, "but I pray you, sleep with me, my Loved One, according to your own counsel in that other book of Solomon: 'If two sleep together they will keep each other warm' (Qoheleth 4:11). Then your presence and the fire of your love will keep my heart even more wide awake and vigilant. It is when your love is burning vigorously within it that my heart keeps watch.

"I lie asleep in order not to disturb my Lover's rest, but the ecstasy in my heart keeps me awake. As I lie in sweet repose, my unsleeping care for you makes me all the more watchful for you in my dreams. O sweet sleep, sweet dreams! To be conscious of nothing else but you, to be still and gaze upon you, though here below the sight of you is granted only in shadow and obscurity, as in a dream!"

How blessed and virtuous is this spiritual intoxication that gives us time and opportunity to contemplate our Loved One! Yet, what we see has a dreamlike quality, because this kind of vision is not the result of human will or effort, nor of any searching on our part; it is something that dawns upon us like a visitation from heaven.

Moreover, the Bride is wise to keep watch, since she does not know when her Lover will come. But constant as her vigil is, so also is the voice of her Lover calling to her. "My heart keeps watch," she says; then she at once goes on to declare: "I hear my Lover knocking and calling out 'Open to me!' Wide awake is my heart, and so too is my Lover's. He knocks at my heart, demanding admittance. Because my heart is awake, he immediately comes close and speaks to me. I recognize his voice; how I love to hear it! To any other voice I am deaf, but his rouses me instantly. The moment my ears catch the sound of it I am transported with joy."

Whose voice can be compared with the voice of Jesus? His teaching and precepts comprise the sum total of perfection, and his voice has the power to stir its hearers to the heart. It penetrates like a two-edged sword (Hebrews 4:12), enabling his message to flow into the heart with a gentle persuasion such as no other teaching has ever been able to command. He makes no high-sounding speeches, yet his words reveal the deep mystery of the Godhead.

In times past God spoke to our ancestors through the prophets, but in these last days he has spoken to us through his Son (Hebrews 1:2), with the strong, powerful accents of a lover.

I Sing of My Lover

*H*ow does your lover differ from any other,
O most beautiful among women?
How does your Lover differ from any other,
that you adjure us so?
My Lover is white and ruddy; he stands out among thousands.
His head is finest gold.
His locks are curled and black as a raven.
His eyes are like doves beside springs of running waters;
they are bathed with milk and set by most abundant springs.
His cheeks are like beds of aromatic spice laid out by the perfumer.
His lips are lilies; they drip with choice myrrh.
His arms are well shaped and golden, adorned with jewels.
His body is a work of ivory inlaid with sapphires.
His legs are columns of marble set in sockets of gold.
His stature like the Lebanon, imposing as the cedars.
His mouth is sweetness itself; he is altogether desirable.
Such is my Lover and such my Friend, Daughters of Jerusalem.
Where has your Loved One gone, O fairest among women?
Which way has your Loved One turned, that we may seek him
    with you?
My Loved One has gone down to his garden, to the beds of spices,
to pasture in the gardens, to gather lilies.
I am my Loved One's and my Loved One is mine,
he who pastures among the lilies.

—*Song of Songs 5:9–6:3*

"His head is finest gold.
His locks are curled and black as a raven."

His hand is finest gold.
His Locks are curled
And black as a RAVEN.
5:11

I Sing of My Lover

*H*ow does my Lover differ from any other? Let me count the ways. No—they are beyond all counting. It will be my delightful eternal task—not to count but to delight in every least facet of this most beautiful of the sons of men (Psalm 45:2). "Words flow out from what fills the heart" (Matthew 12:34). "Lord, who is like you?" (Exodus 15:11).

It is my turn now to sing of my Lover, from his golden toes to his lustrous locks. Black they are, these locks; they hide such mystery. They entice me. How I would love to run my hands through them, to explore their mystery, to let their sensuous softness send currents of ecstatic love through my whole being. Their abundance curls about, so rich is the mystery. They entwine my fingers and seek to hold me fast. They invite me to an intimate communion, face to face.

Let not his golden sheen put you off. In speaking of her Lover, the Beloved rightly begins with what is preeminent, with what is most expressive of the beauty of her Lover: his "head of finest gold." In this she seems to say little. Yet, in that little she speaks of what is most sublime, what is most important, what means the most to her. Its richness bespeaks the richness that lies within. His is not the golden head of Nebuchadnezzar's idol (Daniel 2:32). Rather, it is the gold most precious, the most precious of all, full of light, weighty and solid. It is the gold of love. Is not this the gold we all desire? He who is all love tells me: "You are wretched, pitiably poor, blind naked. Therefore I counsel you, buy from me gold refined by fire, that you may be rich" (Revelation 3:17–18). "You who have no money, come; come and buy without money and without cost" (Isaiah 55:1). This great King is the richest and most generous. No bronze or any other base metal here, only the finest gold. His love for us is indeed the finest: exceedingly lofty, extravagantly rich, wonderfully patient, possessing all the dignity of his majesty. His overwhelming sweetness ensnares us.

He is without doubt the most beautiful of the sons of men (Psalm 45:2), this Son of God. Ravishing is his beauty. Yet, his golden visage and his abundant locks are but an invitation, a presentment of what lies within. Those lily lips, moist with sweetness, invite to a mouth that is sweetness itself. How can I hold back? My whole being yearns for him. Ever and again my soul cries out: Kiss me with the Kiss of your lips.

I am drawn. I am drawn. Let those eyes open to bathe me with their loving gaze. When my Lover looks upon me I am cleansed of all my sordidness. With his loving glances the abundance of his grace washes me clean. I am restored to the innocence of a little one nourished by maternal milk.

Truly, as I look upon him, what can I say? My eyes search every facet of his rich beauty, and I am filled with delight. His hair, his eyes, his cheeks, his lips—they captivate not just the eye but all the senses. I am totally embraced by the aroma of love. His powerful arms: how I long for their embrace. His manly body, strong and lean: how I would press against it until we are melded into one. There is no one as tall and stately as he. Words in chaotic abundance flow forth from me. Color and odor, the allure of spicy gardens, yet all so much richer than the extravagant richness of imperial jewelers: gold and ivory and imported marbles, gems of every sort, sparkling in every crevice. So much nonsense, isn't all this babbling? He is altogether desirable. I can say nothing more.

O raven-black locks, I would hide in your darkness. I know my unworthiness. Yet, I long to be so close. My Lover pastures in the gardens to gather the lilies. No great lily among thorns am I, grounded in humility, trumpeting forth the glory of the

Lord. I am but a very humble lily of the valley; thwarted is my growth. Surely I can be hidden within his dark curls. Uplifted, uplifted by all his vital energy.

But that would not be enough for me: to be entwined in the mysteries of his love, to be lodged close to his sweet lips. Maybe I can dare to give voice to the deepest and strongest aspirations of my lowly being: Kiss me with the Kiss of your lips. And then I will be able to say with all truth: I am my Loved One's and my Loved One is mine.

The Ravishing Beauty of the Beloved

You are as beautiful as Tirzah, my Beloved, as beautiful as Jerusalem,
as awe-inspiring as bannered troops.
Turn your eyes from me, for they torment me.
Your hair is like a flock of goats streaming down Mount Gilead.
Your teeth are like the flock of shorn ewes,
which come up from the washing,
all of them big with twins, none of them barren.
Your cheek is like a half-pomegranate behind your veil.
There are sixty queens, eighty concubines, and maidens without number.
One alone is my dove, my perfect one, her mother's chosen,
the dear one of her parent.
The daughters saw her and declared her most blest,
the queens and concubines, and they sang her praises:
"Who is this that comes forth like the dawn,
as beautiful as the moon, as resplendent as the sun,
as awe-inspiring as bannered troops?"
I went down to the nut orchard, to look at the blossoms of the valley,
to see whether the vines had budded,
whether the pomegranates were in bloom.
Before I was aware, my fancy set me in a chariot beside Amminadib.
Return, return, O Shulammite! Return, return, that we may look upon you.
Why should you look upon the Shulammite
as upon a dance before two armies?

—*Song of Songs 6:4–13*

"Your hair is like a flock of goats streaming down Mount Gilead."

Your hair is like a flock of goats streaming down Mount GILEAD. 4:1

The Ravishing Beauty
of the Beloved

O you of the sinless One, worthy of the tabernacle, woven to veil the All Holy (Exodus 25:4, 26:7), you come to us as an animal marked for sacrifice, a sin offering (Leviticus 9:3) down Gilead, hill of witness, which Jacob made sacred. An estranged son-in-law made his peace with the pursuing Father (Genesis 31). May we too make a peace with the ever-pursuing Divine Lover, giving ourselves to the ravishing touch of the softest of hairs, as long as eternity.

As fragrant as the balm of Gilead that sweetened Joseph's exile journey (Genesis 37:25–28) is your erotic touch that turns life into love, freeing us from all that weighs us down, all that holds us back from the divine ascents.

Mount Gilead, fabled land of richness, mountain forests, and fruitful pastures, feeding all of life (Micah 7:14). Is not this the place of Divine Union, of heaven blessing earth, of earth bursting forth in abundance of life? Here is the place of encounter. Encounter—but not always peaceful: frontier land, nations clashing, our sinfulness seeking to conquer, our pride has to be pierced and ripped.

Has not God more than once repented his creation? The Divine Lover knows the unfaithful one. May we shed our fearsome defenses, our sharp protective horns and ascend the mountain of abundance, bringing to the Lord only our hair of ravishing delight. Defenseless, totally open to the invasion of the Divine, we will be ravished.

The overflowing effusions of Divine Grace stream down upon us, the Divine's creature, to delight, to entice. And yes, even to tear us, to rip open the façades of the false, to let the poison pour out. For only the pure of heart shall see God.

The Divine Grace ever streams down in forms and shapes never expected. Moments of delight, even for climbers who know the burden and sweat of the climb. Gilead reaches to the heavens. We cannot cease to climb. The one who goes not up, goes down.

We go up, up the ascent—each day's step. Dare we lift our eyes to the summit? For hope—yes! But how easily might its wondrous loftiness, as wondrous as it is, cast us down into despair. Who can aspire to such heights: nuptials with the Divine, eternal embraces. Our whole being longs for this. Deep within we know this is what we are made for. Yet, it is so far beyond us.

We humbly bring our eyes down to the now—as we know it. And behold, along the rough terrain, among the rocks and briars: the goats. The longhaired goats, the graces of our Loved One.

Can we rest, dare we rest for a moment, and let them come near? While we rush on, all taken up with our own strivings—even busily helping others, perhaps very needy fellow climbers—we can hardly perceive this visage streaming down from on high. And certainly there is no time to let the goats, the graces of our Loved One, shyly approach, come so close that their long hair can wipe our sweaty brow, stimulate our dormant senses, and put us in touch with our deepest desires, the true meaning of all our striving.

Even the while they assure us of the immediate care and love and presence of our Beloved. For this we must pause, no matter how forcefully our inner desire would impel us on, no matter how loud, how pitiful, how insistent are the cries of the needy around us. If we do not pause, if we do not let ourselves be cared for, how can we help others and care for them—not just in some immediate superficial way but in the way that will respond to their own deepest needs and aspirations? Who has the words of eternal life? Who knows the touch of the Divine?

We pause. We let the longhaired goats draw near. Does their size suddenly frighten us? Their long and sharp horns? Will they overwhelm us? Will they pierce and rip? Who can stand and let the Divine approach?

But are we hearing correctly? Do we have the direction aright? What does the Divine say to us here? For if we take up the text and listen, we hear that it is the Divine Bridegroom, the Lover, who speaks to us, the Beloved:

You are as beautiful as Tirzah, my Beloved....
Turn your eyes from me, for they torment me.
Your hair is like a flock of goats
streaming down Mount Gilead.

Look again: the long hair may indeed stream down, but the goats strive upward toward the crown, the Source, the fulfillment. Beyond the words is the wonder of the Reality, hidden by Seraph's wings but luminously breaking forth. Lofty? Totally beyond us, beyond even the Divine Word of the Revelation. Who can stand at the sight of such a vision? We look up. Yes. And from the Source the hairs of grace stream down. If we let ourselves be aware of their current, their flow will embrace us. And we will be drawn inexorably on.

And it is as the Loved One says to us: Your hair is like a flock of goats.... The Grace of the Divine Hair does not just embrace us, stimulate us, fill us with hope, draw us on. It enters into us. It unites with us. It becomes our life. "I live, now not I, but the Divine lives in me" (Galatians 2:20).

I wonder if there is any truth in Revelation that is more difficult for us to really and effectively accept than this: That we can ravish the Divine. That we can cause ecstatic delight in the Loved One, the delight that these poetic utterances seek to express.

Awaken Not Love

*H*ow graceful are your feet in sandals, Daughter of the Prince!
The curves of your thighs like ornaments, the work of a master
    hand.
Your navel is a rounded bowl that never lacks mixed wine.
Your belly a mound of wheat, encircled by lilies.
Your two breasts are like two fawns, twins of a gazelle.
Your neck is like an ivory tower.
Your eyes are the pools in Heshbon, by the gate of Bath-Rabbim.
Your nose is like a tower of Lebanon, that looks toward Damascus.
Your head crowns you like Carmel,
and your flowing locks are the purple of a king held captive in your
    tresses.
How fair and pleasant you are and how pleasing, dearest One, in
    your delights.
You are stately as a palm tree, and your breasts are like its clusters.
I said, I will climb the palm tree and lay hold of its fruit.
Your breasts are like clusters of the vine, and the scent of your
    breath like apples.
Your mouth is like the best wine, worthy for a loved one to drink,
moistening the lips of sleepers.
I am my Loved One's, and his desire is for me.
Come, my Loved One, let us go forth into the fields, let us abide in
    the villages.
Let us go out early to the vineyards, and see whether the vines have
    budded,

whether the grape blossoms have opened and the pomegranates are
in bloom.
There I will give you my love.
The mandrakes give forth fragrance,
and over our doors are all choice fruits, new as well as old,
which I have laid up for you, my Loved One.
Who will give you to me as my brother, nursed at my mother's
breast,
so that I might meet you outside and kiss you and no one would
despise me?
I would take hold of you and bring you into the house of my
mother.
There you will teach me.
I will give you a cup of spiced wine and the juice of my pomegranates.
His left hand under my head, and his right shall embrace me!
I adjure you, Daughters of Jerusalem,
do not arouse, do not awaken love until it pleases.

—Song of Songs 7:1–8:4

Awaken Not Love

(John of Ford, *Sermons on the Song of Songs*, 99:1–2)

"*I*adjure you, Daughters of Jerusalem, do not arouse, do not awaken love until it pleases." The Lover's words are those of a man passionately in love, of one neither willing nor able to conceal the passion of his love. He is in his bedroom, sleeping with his Bride, and while he has troops of watchmen to guard the city and stand sentry outside the holy palace, he deigns to be, as it were, the one watchman who keeps watch over his Bride. He has surrendered wholly to the delight he finds in her, he has made her wholly ripe for his embraces, and he adjures no one to interrupt, no one to break in upon, no one to disturb this crowning joy of his. Yes, he adjures the Daughters of Jerusalem not to arouse the Beloved or make her awake—that is, not to harass her, however gently, and not to disquiet, however forcefully. When we are first aroused, sleep is not completely shaken off, and we take with us the remnants of our sleep as if we were still dreaming. In fact, we are watching but not yet fully awake. So the Spouse makes it clear he wants the Daughters of Jerusalem to refrain from both kinds of disturbance. They are to keep in mind that the one thing necessary (Luke 10:42), on which the Bride is concentrating, is more important than anything they mean to interrupt her with—and it is Truth who says this.

It is a mighty thing to create heaven and earth, but the work of the Sabbath takes preference over it. It is a great thing to work for the common good and to be the devoted servant of the salvation of many, a task truly salutary and very fruitful. But to gaze silently on the Word is a task literally angelic, or rather divine. The other days, with their tasks, have an evening, but the Sabbath day, with its task—namely, contemplative repose in God—is never brought to an end by evening. All other works, no matter how great a light of salvation they cast upon their day to bring an air of calm, no matter how fully they complete the day's work, suffer an element of obscurity because of the change from light to darkness. And because of their liability to change, they fall short of perfection. But the work of the vision of God and his eternal praise, which is the true work of the Sabbath, never has cloudy weather to dim it and never fades into an evening. No, it is truly a whole without any interval that divides it. It is intensely active without labor, intensely restful without being savorless, and, though final, it is endless.

Of course, God has praise for other works, either that they are good or exceedingly good (Genesis 1:5). But in the judgment of Jesus, Mary's part is the best and therefore will never be taken away from her (Luke 10:42). This is why Scripture tells us that God blessed the seventh day and hallowed it (Genesis 2:3). And he wants you to understand blessing as being endless joy and hallowing as incorruptible holiness. For the true keeping of the Sabbath will be to cleave continually to the blessed sight of our Creator and to be kept by that blessedness from the ability to incur any stain of pride. What a joyful day, what a delightful Sabbath, what a great seventh day.

With You Is All My Wealth

Who is that coming up from the desert,
leaning upon her beloved?
Under the apple tree I awakened you.
There your mother conceived you; there she who bore you was in
    labor.
Set me as a seal upon your heart, as a seal upon your arm;
for love is strong as death, passion fierce as the grave.
Its flashes are flashes of fire, raging flames.
Many waters cannot quench love, nor can floods sweep it away.
If a man offered for love all the wealth of his house, he would be
    utterly scorned.
We have a little sister, and she has no breasts.
What shall we do for our sister on the day she is spoken for?
If she is a wall, we will build upon her a battlement of silver;
but if she is a door, we will enclose her with boards of cedar.
I am a wall and my breasts are towers,
but in his eyes I am one who brings peace.
Solomon had a vineyard at Baal Hamon.
He entrusted the vineyard to keepers;
each one was to bring for its fruit a thousand pieces of silver.
My vineyard, my very own, is for myself.

You, Solomon, may have the thousand, and the keepers of the fruit
  two hundred!
You who dwell in the gardens,
my companions are listening for your voice;
let me hear it.
Flee, my Loved One;
be like a gazelle or a young stag upon the mountains of spices!

—Song of Songs 8:5–14

With You Is All My Wealth

(John of Ford, *Sermons on the Song of Songs*, 110:1, 9–10)

"*I*f a man offered for love all the wealth of his house, he would be utterly scorned." A good line on which to end the Bride's praises. Up to the present, the Spouse has preached with eloquence and force about the virtues of charity. Now he concludes by saying the height of these virtues is subsumed under the law of poverty and humility. "If a man offered for love all the wealth of his house," he tells us, "he would be utterly scorned." In these words, the beauty of true poverty seems to be very clearly put before us, so that now, one can only consider oneself truly one of Christ's poor when one has offered all the wealth of one's house for love.

The man of whom the Spouse is speaking, since he has given all the wealth of his house for love: not merely the wealth he is seen to possess externally, but that with which he abounds within—and that is much more difficult to reject—he will despise it as nothing. For something of little account begins to seem worthless when compared with something great; indeed, the lack of any true comparison leads him to think it nothing. It is so very unlike that it is no longer even taken into account. First, there is "utter scorn" for whatever worldly pleasures the world finds desirable, and then for whatever a man finds lovable in his own self-will. Instead of all these things, the love of Christ begins to take possession of us and to be possessed, and it becomes the true riches and wealth of this house, though the house is not big enough for it.

All the wealth that I possess apart from this is as nothing in your sight, Lord God (Psalm 39:5). Oh, if only I could see it exactly as you see it, then I could utterly scorn it for the sake of your love and in comparison with your love. One day you alone will become my portion. Then I will glory in you alone and claim that "with you is all my wealth" (Psalm 39:7). When I am with you, I shall be rich because of you, since I would have been poor indeed, relying on myself. I shall be all the more truly totally all yours the more profoundly I cease to be all mine. As far as my will is concerned, may it all be turned into your will, so that from now on, my will may not be called my will, but your will should take its place. This means that my soul will be blissfully married to you, her lawful Spouse, reverently and humbly united to you by the full consent of a pure will.

Gladly and willingly it is my intention to have the wealth of my will transformed into the rich wealth of your will, and not only my will but whatever understanding there is in my mind and whatever meditations and desires there are in my memory. But you must help my strivings, Lord, or I shall labor in vain.

Afterword: In Love with the Bible

alling in love at first sight is exactly what happened with
me and the Bible. Starting Hebrew School at about nine
years old, I was mesmerized by every figure and adventure in
this astonishing Book. It could never have occurred to me then
or even later that I could make a life's work out of a volume five
thousand years old. After more than twenty years of teaching,
and of building my reputation as an artist with the eventual
project of creating more than forty pieces of sculpture for permanent placement at Ellis Island and five bronzes standing per-
manently at the base of the Statue of Liberty, I was ready to
pursue my life's dream.

The stories of Genesis and Exodus continued to intoxicate
my imagination and eventually culminated in the establish-
ment of two museums, one in Israel and one in America, on the
theme of the Bible. The museums are the Israel Bible Museum
in Safed, Israel, and the Dennis & Phillip Ratner Museum in
suburban Washington, D.C.

It was not until my forties that I began to understand and
appreciate what Judaism calls "The Writings." Ecclesiastes,
Psalms, Job, and the Song of Songs demand more life experi-
ences for a true appreciation of them. Each of these has been
source material for my work. It took another stage of my life to
enable me to deal with the Song of Songs, and that was a
mature, passionate, and deep love. That occurred in my forty-
seventh year, when I met my wife and proposed the night that
I met her. Although this sounds much like a romance novel, it
continues to this day. I come to the Song of Songs with full
knowledge of the sacred, spiritual, and sensual awareness of
human love in a covenant relationship. The imagery presented

in words is so magnificent that my concepts become realized immediately, and yet one line produces many works. Some of the pieces in this volume were produced in America and some in the Holy Land and span years, not months. This volume contains only a portion of what the Song of Songs has inspired me to create. It was Abbot Basil Pennington's visit to the Dennis & Phillip Ratner Museum one afternoon that instigated the union of his writing and my art. I hope this is the first such collaboration uniting us in the bounty of possibilities presented by the Book of Books.

—Phillip Ratner

The Cistercian Commentary
on the Song of Songs

*T*he New Monastery, which gave birth to the Cistercian Order, was founded at Citeaux in 1098 to renew monastic life through a fuller living of Benedict of Nursia's *Rule for Monasteries*. The contemplative dimension of the Cistercian monks' life was inspired and nourished in a special way by the Song of Songs.

The primary master of the Cistercian school of spirituality was Bernard of Clairvaux. Born at Dijon, France, in 1090, Bernard gave himself to prayer and study, unlike his knightly brothers. However, when he entered Citeaux in 1112, he brought thirty relatives with him, including all his brothers (the youngest brother and his father came a bit later). Given his leadership abilities, three years later Bernard was sent to establish the Abbey of Clairvaux. In the course of the next thirty-eight years he sent forth monks to establish or reform hundreds of monasteries in all parts of Christendom. In 1145 one of his spiritual sons was elected pope. In 1135 Bernard began commenting on the Song of Songs; by the time he died, in 1153, he had published eighty-six sermons, bringing him up to the third chapter of the Song.

Gilbert of Hoyland, a disciple of Bernard of Clairvaux, became abbot of Swineshead, on the eastern coast of England, a few years before the latter's death. We know relatively little of this monk, although he was, like his mentor, certainly a monk of deep spirituality, well educated and a fine writer. His claim to fame comes from his having taken up the commentary on the Song of Songs from where Bernard left off. Before he died in 1172 Gilbert had completed forty-eight sermons and had reached the fifth chapter of the Song, verse ten.

Again, we know little of the early life of John, the abbot of Bindon in Dorset, who was elected to the seat at Ford Abbey in Devon in 1192. He was inspired to take up the commentary on the Song of Songs where Gilbert left off, and before his death in 1214 he completed it in the course of 120 sermons. Like Gilbert, John explicitly followed in the footsteps of Saint Bernard; like Bernard and the Cistercians in general, John was well aware of and studied in the rich tradition that went before them and is a channel through which it comes to us.

Suggested Reading

The Song of Songs. Arranged and edited by Frederick W. Bassett. Brewster, Mass.: Paraclete Press, 2002.

The Song of Songs. Translated with an introduction and commentary by Ariel Bloch and Chana Bloch. Berkeley: University of California Press, 1995.

Astell, Ann W. *The Song of Songs in the Middle Ages.* Ithaca: Cornell University Press, 1990.

Bernard of Clairvaux. *A Lover Teaching the Way of Love: Selected Writings.* Introduced and edited by M. Basil Pennington. Hyde Park, N.Y.: New City Press, 1997.

———. *Love Songs: Wisdom from Saint Bernard of Clairvaux.* Edited by Jeanne Kun. Ijamsville, Md.: The Word Among Us, 2001.

———. *On the Song of Songs.* Translated by Kilian Walsh and Irene Edmonds. 4 vols. Spencer, Mass.: Cistercian Publications, 1971–1980.

———. *Talks on the Song of Songs.* Edited and Modernized by Bernard Bangley. Brewster, Mass.: Paraclete Press, 2002.

Casey, Michael. *Athirst for God: Spiritual Desire in Bernard of Clairvaux's Sermons on the Song of Songs.* Kalamazoo, Mich.: Cistercian Publications, 1987.

Garrett, Duane. *World Biblical Commentary.* Vol. 23B: Song of Songs. Nashville: Thomas Nelson, 2004.

Gershom (Gersonides), Levi ben. *Commentary on the Song of Songs.* Translated with introduction and annotations by Menachem Kellner. New Haven: Yale University Press, 1998.

Gilbert of Hoyland. *Sermons on the Song of Songs.* Translated by Lawrence C. Braceland. 3 vols. Kalamazoo, Mich.: Cistercian Publications, 1978–1979.

Glendhill, Tom. *The Message of the Song of Songs: The Lyrics of Love.* Downers Grove, Ill.: InterVarsity Press, 1994.

Guyon, Jeanne. *Song of Songs.* New Kensington, Pa.: Whitaker House, 1997.

John of Ford. *Sermons on the Final Verses of the Song of Songs.* Translated by Sister Wendy Beckett. 7 vols. Kalamazoo, Mich.: Cistercian Publications, 1977–1984.

Kell, Othmar. *The Song of Songs: A Continental Commentary.* Translated by Frederick J. Gaiser. Minneapolis: Fortress Press, 1994.

William of St. Thierry. *Exposition on the Song of Songs.* Translated by Columba Hart. Spencer, Mass.: Cistercian Publications, 1970.

———. *The Way of Divine Union. Selected Writings.* Introduced and edited by M. Basil Pennington. Hyde Park, N.Y.: New City Press, 1998.

About SKYLIGHT PATHS Publishing

SkyLight Paths Publishing is creating a place where people of different spiritual traditions come together for challenge and inspiration, a place where we can help each other understand the mystery that lies at the heart of our existence.

Through spirituality, our religious beliefs are increasingly becoming a part of our lives—rather than *apart* from our lives. While many of us may be more interested than ever in spiritual growth, we may be less firmly planted in traditional religion. Yet, we do want to deepen our relationship to the sacred, to learn from our own as well as from other faith traditions, and to practice in new ways.

SkyLight Paths sees both believers and seekers as a community that increasingly transcends traditional boundaries of religion and denomination—people wanting to learn from each other, *walking together, finding the way.*

We at SkyLight Paths take great care to produce beautiful books that present meaningful spiritual content in a form that reflects the art of making high quality books. Therefore, we want to acknowledge those who contributed to the production of this book.

PRODUCTION
Tim Holtz

EDITORIAL
Lauren Seidman & Emily Wichland

JACKET DESIGN
Tim Holtz

TEXT DESIGN
Lisa Buckley, Lisa Buckley Design, San Francisco

PRINTING & BINDING
Friesens Corporation, Manitoba, Canada

Other Interesting Books—Spirituality

Lighting the Lamp of Wisdom: *A Week Inside a Yoga Ashram*
by *John Ittner;* Foreword by *Dr. David Frawley*

This insider's guide to Hindu spiritual life takes you into a typical week of retreat inside a yoga ashram to demystify the experience and show you what to expect from your own visit. Includes a discussion of worship services, meditation and yoga classes, chanting and music, work practice, and more.

6 x 9, 192 pp, b/w photographs, Quality PB, ISBN 1-893361-52-7 **$15.95**; HC, ISBN 1-893361-37-3 **$24.95**

Waking Up: *A Week Inside a Zen Monastery*
by *Jack Maguire;* Foreword by *John Daido Loori, Roshi*

An essential guide to what it's like to spend a week inside a Zen Buddhist monastery.

6 x 9, 224 pp, b/w photographs, Quality PB, ISBN 1-893361-55-1 **$16.95**; HC, ISBN 1-893361-13-6 **$21.95**

Making a Heart for God: *A Week Inside a Catholic Monastery*
by *Dianne Aprile;* Foreword by *Brother Patrick Hart,* ocso

This essential guide to experiencing life in a Catholic monastery takes you to the Abbey of Gethsemani—the Trappist monastery in Kentucky that was home to author Thomas Merton—to explore the details. "More balanced and informative than the popular *The Cloister Walk* by Kathleen Norris." —*Choice: Current Reviews for Academic Libraries*

6 x 9, 224 pp, b/w photographs, Quality PB, ISBN 1-893361-49-7 **$16.95**; HC, ISBN 1-893361-14-4 **$21.95**

Come and Sit: *A Week Inside Meditation Centers*
by *Marcia Z. Nelson;* Foreword by *Wayne Teasdale*

The insider's guide to meditation in a variety of different spiritual traditions. Traveling through Buddhist, Hindu, Christian, Jewish, and Sufi traditions, this essential guide takes you to different meditation centers to meet the teachers and students and learn about the practices, demystifying the meditation experience.

6 x 9, 224 pp, b/w photographs, Quality PB, ISBN 1-893361-35-7 **$16.95**

Or phone, fax, mail or e-mail to: SKYLIGHT PATHS Publishing
Sunset Farm Offices, Route 4 • P.O. Box 237 • Woodstock, Vermont 05091
Tel: (802) 457-4000 • Fax: (802) 457-4004 • www.skylightpaths.com
Credit card orders: (800) 962-4544 (8:30AM–5:30PM ET Monday–Friday)
Generous discounts on quantity orders. SATISFACTION GUARANTEED. Prices subject to change.

Spiritual Practice

The Sacred Art of Bowing
Preparing to Practice
by *Andi Young*

This informative and inspiring introduction to bowing—and related spiritual practices—shows you how to do it, why it's done, and what spiritual benefits it has to offer. Incorporates interviews, personal stories, illustrations of bowing in practice, advice on how you can incorporate bowing into your daily life, and how bowing can deepen spiritual understanding.
5½ x 8½, 128 pp, b/w illus., Quality PB, ISBN 1-893361-82-9 **$14.95**

Praying with Our Hands: *Twenty-One Practices of Embodied Prayer from the World's Spiritual Traditions*
by *Jon M. Sweeney*; Photographs by *Jennifer J. Wilson*;
Foreword by *Mother Tessa Bielecki*; Afterword by *Taitetsu Unno, PhD*

A spiritual guidebook for bringing prayer into our bodies.
This inspiring book of reflections and accompanying photographs shows us twenty-one simple ways of using our hands to speak to God, to enrich our devotion and ritual. All express the various approaches of the world's religious traditions to bringing the body into worship. Spiritual traditions represented include Anglican, Sufi, Zen, Roman Catholic, Yoga, Shaker, Hindu, Jewish, Pentecostal, Eastern Orthodox, and many others.
8 x 8, 96 pp, 22 duotone photographs, Quality PB, ISBN 1-893361-16-0 **$16.95**

 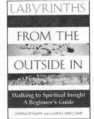

The Sacred Art of Listening
Forty Reflections for Cultivating a Spiritual Practice
by *Kay Lindahl*; Illustrations by *Amy Schnapper*

More than ever before, we need to embrace the skills and practice of listening. You will learn to: Speak clearly from your heart • Communicate with courage and compassion • Heighten your awareness for deep listening • Enhance your ability to listen to people with different belief systems. 8 x 8, 160 pp, Illus., Quality PB, ISBN 1-893361-44-6 **$16.99**

Labyrinths from the Outside In
Walking to Spiritual Insight—A Beginner's Guide
by *Donna Schaper* and *Carole Ann Camp*

The user-friendly, interfaith guide to making and using labyrinths— for meditation, prayer, and celebration.
Labyrinth walking is a spiritual exercise *anyone* can do. This accessible guide unlocks the mysteries of the labyrinth for all of us, providing ideas for using the labyrinth walk for prayer, meditation, and celebrations to mark the most important moments in life. Includes instructions for making a labyrinth of your own and finding one in your area.
6 x 9, 208 pp, b/w illus. and photographs, Quality PB, ISBN 1-893361-18-7 **$16.95**

SkyLight Illuminations Series
Andrew Harvey, series editor

Offers today's spiritual seeker an enjoyable entry into the great classic texts of the world's spiritual traditions. Each classic is presented in an accessible translation, with facing pages of guided commentary from experts, giving you the keys you need to understand the history, context, and meaning of the text. This series enables readers of all backgrounds to experience and understand classic spiritual texts directly, and to make them a part of their lives. Andrew Harvey writes the foreword to each volume, an insightful, personal introduction to each classic.

Bhagavad Gita: *Annotated & Explained*
Translation by *Shri Purohit Swami;* Annotation by *Kendra Crossen Burroughs*
"The very best Gita for first-time readers." —Ken Wilber

Millions of people turn daily to India's most beloved holy book, whose universal appeal has made it popular with non-Hindus and Hindus alike. This edition introduces you to the characters, explains references and philosophical terms, shares the interpretations of famous spiritual leaders and scholars, and more. 5½ x 8½, 192 pp, Quality PB, ISBN 1-893361-28-4 **$16.95**

The Way of a Pilgrim: *Annotated & Explained*
Translation and annotation by *Gleb Pokrovsky*

This classic of Russian spirituality is the delightful account of one man who sets out to learn the prayer of the heart—also known as the "Jesus prayer"—and how the practice transforms his life. 5½ x 8½, 160 pp, Illus., Quality PB, ISBN 1-893361-31-4 **$14.95**

The Gospel of Thomas: *Annotated & Explained*
Translation and annotation by *Stevan Davies*

Discovered in 1945, this collection of aphoristic sayings sheds new light on the origins of Christianity and the intriguing figure of Jesus, portraying the Kingdom of God as a present fact about the world, rather than a future promise or future threat. This edition guides you through the text with annotations that focus on the meaning of the sayings. 5½ x 8½, 192 pp, Quality PB, ISBN 1-893361-45-4 **$16.95**

Rumi and Islam: *Selections from His Stories, Poems, and Discourses—Annotated & Explained*
Translation and annotation by *Ibrahim Gamard*

Offers a new way of thinking about Rumi's poetry. Ibrahim Gamard focuses on Rumi's place within the Sufi tradition of Islam, providing you with insight into the mystical side of the religion—one that has love of God at its core and sublime wisdom teachings as its pathways. 5½ x 8½, 240 pp, Quality PB, ISBN 1-59473-002-4 **$15.99**

SkyLight Illuminations Series

Andrew Harvey, series editor

Zohar: *Annotated & Explained*
Translation and annotation by *Daniel C. Matt*

The cornerstone text of Kabbalah.

The best-selling author of *The Essential Kabbalah* brings together in one place the most important teachings of the *Zohar*, the canonical text of Jewish mystical tradition. Guides you step by step through the midrash, mystical fantasy, and Hebrew scripture that make up the *Zohar*, explaining the inner meanings in facing-page commentary. Ideal for readers without any prior knowledge of Jewish mysticism.

5½ x 8½, 176 pp, Quality PB, ISBN 1-893361-51-9 **$15.99**

Selections from the Gospel of Sri Ramakrishna
Annotated & Explained
Translation by *Swami Nikhilananda*; Annotation by *Kendra Crossen Burroughs*

The words of India's greatest example of God-consciousness and mystical ecstasy in recent history.

Introduces the fascinating world of the Indian mystic and the universal appeal of his message that has inspired millions of devotees for more than a century. Selections from the original text and insightful yet unobtrusive commentary highlight the most important and inspirational teachings. Ideal for readers without any prior knowledge of Hinduism.

5½ x 8½, 240 pp, b/w photographs, Quality PB, ISBN 1-893361-46-2 **$16.95**

Dhammapada: *Annotated & Explained*
Translation by *Max Müller* and revised by *Jack Maguire*; Annotation by *Jack Maguire*

The classic of Buddhist spiritual practice.

The Dhammapada—words spoken by the Buddha himself over 2,500 years ago—is notoriously difficult to understand for the first-time reader. Now you can experience it with understanding even if you have no previous knowledge of Buddhism. Enlightening facing-page commentary explains all the names, terms, and references, giving you deeper insight into the text.

5½ x 8½, 160 pp, b/w photographs, Quality PB, ISBN 1-893361-42-X **$14.95**

Hasidic Tales: *Annotated & Explained*
Translation and annotation by *Rabbi Rami Shapiro*

The legendary tales of the impassioned Hasidic rabbis.

The allegorical quality of Hasidic tales can be perplexing. Here, they are presented as stories rather than parables, making them accessible and meaningful. Each demonstrates the spiritual power of unabashed joy, offers lessons for leading a holy life, and reminds us that the Divine can be found in the everyday. Annotations explain theological concepts, introduce major characters, and clarify references unfamiliar to most readers.

5½ x 8½, 240 pp, Quality PB, ISBN 1-893361-86-1 **$16.95**

Meditation/Prayer

Finding Grace at the Center: *The Beginning of Centering Prayer*

by *M. Basil Pennington, OCSO, Thomas Keating, OCSO, and Thomas E. Clarke, SJ*

The book that helped launch the Centering Prayer "movement." Explains the prayer of *The Cloud of Unknowing*, posture and relaxation, the three simple rules of centering prayer, and how to cultivate centering prayer throughout all aspects of your life.

5 x 7¼,112 pp, HC, ISBN 1-893361-69-1 **$14.95**

Prayers to an Evolutionary God

by *William Cleary;* Afterword by *Diarmuid O'Murchu*

How is it possible to pray when God is dislocated from heaven, dispersed all around us, and more of a creative force than an all-knowing father? In this unique collection of eighty prose prayers and related commentary, William Cleary considers new ways of thinking about God and the world around us. Inspired by the spiritual and scientific teachings of Diarmuid O'Murchu and Teilhard de Chardin, Cleary reveals that religion and science can be combined to create an expanding view of the universe—an evolutionary faith.

6 x 9, 208 pp, HC, ISBN 1-59473-006-7 **$21.99**

Meditation without Gurus
A Guide to the Heart of Practice

by *Clark Strand*

Short, compelling reflections show you how to make meditation a part of your daily life, without the complication of gurus, mantras, retreats, or treks to distant mountains. This enlightening book strips the practice down to its essential heart—simplicity, lightness, and peace—showing you that the most important part of practice is not whether you can get in the full lotus position, but rather your ability to become fully present in the moment.

5½ x 8½, 192 pp, Quality PB, ISBN 1-893361-93-4 **$16.95**

Meditation & Its Practices
A Definitive Guide to Techniques and Traditions of Meditation in Yoga and Vedanta

by *Swami Adiswarananda*

The complete sourcebook for exploring Hinduism's two most time-honored traditions of meditation.

Drawing on both classic and contemporary sources, this comprehensive sourcebook outlines the scientific, psychological, and spiritual elements of Yoga and Vedanta meditation.

6 x 9, 504 pp, HC, ISBN 1-893361-83-7 **$34.95**

Spirituality/History

The Monks of Mount Athos
A Western Monk's Extraordinary Spiritual Journey on Eastern Holy Ground
by M. Basil Pennington, OCSO; Foreword by Archimandrite Dionysios

Experience the soul of the Christian East.

Pennington was the first Western monk to stay on Mount Athos for more than the usual overnight visit. Listen in as he wrestles with theological differences between Christianity's East and West, learns the orthodox practice of "the prayer of the heart," and explores the landscape, the monastic communities, and the food of Athos—a monastic republic like no other place on earth.
6 x 9, 256 pp, 10+ b/w line drawings, Quality PB, ISBN 1-893361-78-0 **$18.95**

Bede Griffiths
An Introduction to His Interspiritual Thought
by Wayne Teasdale

The first in-depth study of Bede Griffiths' contemplative experience and thought.

Wayne Teasdale, a longtime personal friend and student of Griffiths, creates in this intimate portrait an intriguing view into the beliefs and life of this champion of interreligious acceptance and harmony. Explains key terms that form the basis of Griffiths' contemplative understanding, and the essential characteristics of his theology as they relate to the Hindu and Christian traditions.
6 x 9, 288 pp, Quality PB, ISBN 1-893361-77-2 **$18.95**

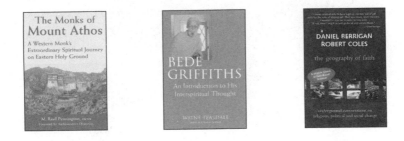

The Geography of Faith
Underground Conversations on Religious, Political and Social Change
by Daniel Berrigan and Robert Coles; Updated introduction and afterword by the authors

A classic of faith-based activism—updated for a new generation.

Listen in on the conversations between these two great teachers—one a renegade priest wanted by the FBI for his protests against the Vietnam war, the other a future Pulitzer Prize-winning journalist—as they struggle with what it means to put your faith to the test. Discover how their story of challenging the status quo during a time of great political, religious, and social change is just as applicable to our lives today. 6 x 9, 224 pp, Quality PB, ISBN 1-893361-40-3 **$16.95**

Religious Etiquette/Reference

How to Be a Perfect Stranger, 3rd Edition
The Essential Religious Etiquette Handbook
Edited by *Stuart M. Matlins* and *Arthur J. Magida*

The indispensable guidebook to help the well-meaning guest when visiting other people's religious ceremonies.

A straightforward guide to the rituals and celebrations of the major religions and denominations in the United States and Canada from the perspective of an interested guest of any other faith, based on information obtained from authorities of each religion. Belongs in every living room, library, and office.

COVERS:

African American Methodist Churches • Assemblies of God • Baha'i • Baptist • Buddhist • Christian Church (Disciples of Christ) • Christian Science (Church of Christ, Scientist) • Churches of Christ • Episcopalian and Anglican • Hindu • Islam • Jehovah's Witnesses • Jewish • Lutheran • Mennonite/Amish • Methodist • Mormon (Church of Jesus Christ of Latter-day Saints) • Native American/First Nations • Orthodox Churches • Pentecostal Church of God • Presbyterian • Quaker (Religious Society of Friends) • Reformed Church in America/Canada • Roman Catholic • Seventh-day Adventist • Sikh • Unitarian Universalist • United Church of Canada • United Church of Christ

6 x 9, 432 pp, Quality PB, ISBN 1-893361-67-5 **$19.95**

What You Will See Inside A Mosque
by *Aisha Karen Khan*; Photographs by *Aaron Pepis*

A colorful, fun-to-read introduction that explains the ways and whys of Muslim faith and worship.

Visual and informative, featuring full-page pictures and concise descriptions of what is happening, the objects used, the spiritual leaders and laypeople who have specific roles, and the spiritual intent of the believers.

Ideal for children as well as teachers, parents, librarians, clergy, and lay leaders who want to demystify the celebrations and ceremonies of Islam throughout the year, as well as encourage understanding and tolerance among different faith traditions.

8½ x 10½, 32 pp, Full-color photographs, HC, ISBN 1-893361-60-8 **$16.95**

Or phone, fax, mail or e-mail to: SKYLIGHT PATHS Publishing

Sunset Farm Offices, Route 4 • P.O. Box 237 • Woodstock, Vermont 05091

Tel: (802) 457-4000 • Fax: (802) 457-4004 • www.skylightpaths.com

Credit card orders: (800) 962-4544 (8:30AM–5:30PM ET Monday–Friday)

Generous discounts on quantity orders. SATISFACTION GUARANTEED. Prices subject to change.